Vincent C. Emeakaroha

Self-Manageable Cloud Service Provisioning Infrastructure

Vincent C. Emeakaroha

Self-Manageable Cloud Service Provisioning Infrastructure

SLA Enforcement via Holistic Monitoring Techniques and Novel Application Scheduling Mechanism

Südwestdeutscher Verlag für Hochschulschriften

Impressum/Imprint (nur für Deutschland/only for Germany)
Bibliografische Information der Deutschen Nationalbibliothek: Die Deutsche Nationalbibliothek verzeichnet diese Publikation in der Deutschen Nationalbibliografie; detaillierte bibliografische Daten sind im Internet über http://dnb.d-nb.de abrufbar.
Alle in diesem Buch genannten Marken und Produktnamen unterliegen warenzeichen-, marken- oder patentrechtlichem Schutz bzw. sind Warenzeichen oder eingetragene Warenzeichen der jeweiligen Inhaber. Die Wiedergabe von Marken, Produktnamen, Gebrauchsnamen, Handelsnamen, Warenbezeichnungen u.s.w. in diesem Werk berechtigt auch ohne besondere Kennzeichnung nicht zu der Annahme, dass solche Namen im Sinne der Warenzeichen- und Markenschutzgesetzgebung als frei zu betrachten wären und daher von jedermann benutzt werden dürften.

Coverbild: www.ingimage.com

Verlag: Südwestdeutscher Verlag für Hochschulschriften GmbH & Co. KG
Heinrich-Böcking-Str. 6-8, 66121 Saarbrücken, Deutschland
Telefon +49 681 37 20 271-1, Telefax +49 681 37 20 271-0
Email: info@svh-verlag.de

Approved by: Wien, Technische Universität, Diss., 2012

Herstellung in Deutschland (siehe letzte Seite)
ISBN: 978-3-8381-3359-1

Imprint (only for USA, GB)
Bibliographic information published by the Deutsche Nationalbibliothek: The Deutsche Nationalbibliothek lists this publication in the Deutsche Nationalbibliografie; detailed bibliographic data are available in the Internet at http://dnb.d-nb.de.
Any brand names and product names mentioned in this book are subject to trademark, brand or patent protection and are trademarks or registered trademarks of their respective holders. The use of brand names, product names, common names, trade names, product descriptions etc. even without a particular marking in this works is in no way to be construed to mean that such names may be regarded as unrestricted in respect of trademark and brand protection legislation and could thus be used by anyone.

Cover image: www.ingimage.com

Publisher: Südwestdeutscher Verlag für Hochschulschriften GmbH & Co. KG
Heinrich-Böcking-Str. 6-8, 66121 Saarbrücken, Germany
Phone +49 681 37 20 271-1, Fax +49 681 37 20 271-0
Email: info@svh-verlag.de

Printed in the U.S.A.
Printed in the U.K. by (see last page)
ISBN: 978-3-8381-3359-1

Copyright © 2012 by the author and Südwestdeutscher Verlag für Hochschulschriften GmbH & Co. KG and licensors
All rights reserved. Saarbrücken 2012

Abstract

Rapid technological developments in Information Technology (IT) and ubiquitous Internet access are causing serious challenges in service provisioning and resource management landscapes. Cloud computing is proving to be a reliable technology to address these challenges. Service provisioning in the Cloud relies on Service Level Agreements (SLAs) representing a contract signed between the customer and the service provider including non-functional requirements of the service specified as Quality of Service (QoS) and penalties in case of violations. Flexible and reliable management of resources and SLA agreements are of paramount importance to both Cloud providers and consumers. On the one hand, providers have to prevent SLA violations to avoid penalties and on the other hand, they have to ensure high resource utilization to prevent costly maintenance of unused resources.

Although, there is a large body of work considering development of flexible and self-manageable Cloud computing infrastructures, there is still a lack of adequate monitoring infrastructures capable of predicting possible SLA violations. Most of the available monitoring systems rely either on Grid or service-oriented infrastructures, which are not directly compatible to Clouds due to the differences in resource usage models, or due to heavily network-oriented monitoring infrastructures.

Furthermore, to achieve high resource utilization and more revenue, the providers must be able to schedule resources and deploy different user applications complying with the SLA objectives, and at the same time optimizing the performance of the applications. The current scheduling approaches in Clouds are tailored toward the usage of single SLA objectives, such as execution time in decision making. The design of a generalized scheduling algorithm for optimal mapping of an application with multiple SLA parameters to resources is yet to be investigated. Nevertheless, the idea of scheduling and deploying multiple applications on the same host brings a new set of challenges to the Cloud provider because he must enforce the SLA terms of each customer application independently.

In this thesis, we propose a novel Cloud management infrastructure, which is based on holistic monitoring techniques and mechanisms for low-level resource metrics to high-level SLA mapping, application scheduling and deployment, and the ability to monitor multiple application executing on the same host. We present the design and implementation of these techniques. In a case study, we show the integration of knowledge management techniques into Cloud management infrastructures realizing autonomic behaviour and providing reactive action to prevent / correct the SLA violation situations. Finally, we present some evaluations to show the novelty of the contributed solutions.

Acknowledgements

This dissertation is the result of my research work at the Distributed System Group (DSG), Information Systems Institute, Vienna University of Technology. The research project through which this work is realized is funded by the Vienna Science and Technology Fund known in German as *Wiener Wissenschafts-, Forschungs- und Technologiefonds (WWTF)* under the grant agreement ICT08-018 Foundations of Self-governing ICT Infrastructures (FoSII).

I would like to express my deepest gratitude to my supervisors *Univ. Prof. Dr. Schahram Dustdar* and *Univ. Ass. Dr. Ivona Brandic* for giving me the opportunity to write this thesis and for their moral support and constructive guidance throughout the work.

A special appreciation goes to my second examiner and collaborator *Univ. Prof. Dr. César A. F. De Rose*. Thank you for collaborating with me on most of my research work and for your quality advice. In addition, thank you also for taking the trouble to come all the way from Brazil to attend my defense examination. At the same time, my gratitude goes to our other collaborators *Dr. Marco A. S. Netto* and *Dr. Rodrigo N. Calheiros*. Thanks a lot for the great work together.

Furthermore, I would like to thank all my colleagues at the DSG especially *DI DI Michael Maurer* and *Ivan Breskovic, MSc.* for their constructive critique and collegial support towards my research work, which helped to improve the quality of this work.

Hearty thanks to my Austrian family of *Gisela & Oliver Prisching* for their hospitality, love, and support all these years. I also remain sincerely grateful to *Oma & Opa Prisching*, *Lucia & Michael Zehndorfer*, *Opa Johann Radlherr & Barbara*, *Marianne & Kurt Zehndorfer*, and *Brigitta & Gehard Kuntner* for their friendship and support. May God bless you all.

My profound gratitude goes to *Miss MMag. Marianne Gruber* for her relentless effort in proof-reading and translating parts of my work, and her care and support in different situations during my studies. I will ever remain grateful.

Finally, I dedicate this work to my whole family especially my parents *Chief Prince & Lady E. O. N Emeakaroha*, brothers, and sisters. Thank you for giving me the opportunity and encouragement to pursue my studies up to this level. May the good Lord bless and protect you all.

Contents

Abstract   i

Acknowledgements   iii

Contents   v

List of Tables   vii

List of Figures   ix

Selected Publications   xi

1 Introduction   1
   1.1 Problem Statement 2
   1.2 Research Questions 4
   1.3 Scientific Contributions 6
   1.4 Thesis Organization 7

2 Background   9
   2.1 FoSII Research Project 9
   2.2 Service Level Agreement 12
   2.3 Autonomic Behaviour 13

3 Cloud Infrastructure Monitoring   15
   3.1 Metrics Monitoring and Mapping Motivation 15
   3.2 LoM2HiS Design Details 17
   3.3 LoM2HiS Implementation Choices 20
   3.4 Applying LoM2HiS to Traffic Management Systems 22
   3.5 DeSVi Architecture Motivation 26
   3.6 DeSVi Design Details 28
   3.7 DeSVi Implementation Strategies 31

4 SLA-Aware Application Scheduling   33
   4.1 Scheduling Approach Motivation 33

	4.2	Resource Provisioning and Application Deployment Models	35
	4.3	Scheduling and Load Balancing Mechanisms	37
	4.4	Implementation Issues	40

5 Cloud Application Monitoring — 43
    5.1 Application Monitoring Motivation 43
    5.2 CASViD Design Concept 44
    5.3 Implementation Choices 48

6 Holistic Monitoring and Management of Provisioning Lifecycle — 51
    6.1 Holistic Monitoring Concept 51
    6.2 Knowledge Management techniques 51
    6.3 Case Study: Integrating Monitoring with Knowledge Management . . 53

7 Evaluation — 61
    7.1 Metrics Monitoring and Mapping Evaluation 61
    7.2 Traffic Management System Monitoring Evaluation 64
    7.3 Resource and SLA Monitoring Evaluation 67
    7.4 SLA-Aware Scheduling Evaluation 77
    7.5 Application Monitoring Evaluation 83
    7.6 Case Study Evaluation 90

8 Related Work — 97
    8.1 Cloud infrastructure Monitoring 97
    8.2 Scheduling Mechanisms 99
    8.3 Application Monitoring in Clouds 101
    8.4 SLA Enforcement and Management 104

9 Conclusion — 107
    9.1 Summary 107
    9.2 Contraints on Thesis Contributions 108
    9.3 Future Work 109

Bibliography — 111

Glossary — 129

List of Tables

2.1	SLA Agreement Example.	12
3.1	Complex Mapping Rules.	20
6.1	Workflow SLA Objectives.	56
7.1	Run-Time Monitor Evaluation Settings.	63
7.2	Cloud Environment Resource Setup Composed of 36 Virtual Machines.	68
7.3	SLA Objective Thresholds for the Three POV-Ray Applications.	70
7.4	Measurement Intervals.	71
7.5	TPCW Experimentation Results.	76
7.6	Cloud Environment Resource Setup	79
7.7	Heterogenous Application SLA Objectives	79
7.8	Scheduler Comparison	82
7.9	SLA Objective Thresholds Specification.	85
7.10	Number of Detected SLA Violations.	86
7.11	Computational Node Capacity	91

List of Figures

2.1	FoSII Infrastructure Overview.	9
2.2	Case-Based Reasoning Process Overview	11
2.3	Case Based-Reasoning Example.	11
3.1	LoM2HiS Motivation Scenario.	16
3.2	LoM2HiS Framework Overview.	17
3.3	Host Monitoring System	18
3.4	Communication Mechanism Overview	21
3.5	Components of a Traffic Management System.	23
3.6	Applying LoM2HiS to TMS.	25
3.7	LoM2HiS Dataflow.	26
3.8	DeSVi Motivating Scenario.	27
3.9	Overview of the DeSVi Architecture and Component's Interaction.	28
3.10	Application Deployer.	29
3.11	Automated Emulation Framework Overview.	30
4.1	Scheduling Motivation Scenario	34
4.2	LoM2HiS with Scheduling Strategy	35
4.3	Cloud Provisioning and Deployment Model.	36
4.4	CloudSim Extension Architecture.	40
5.1	CASViD Motivating Scenario.	44
5.2	CASViD Architecture Overview.	45
5.3	CASViD Monitor Overview.	46
6.1	Knowledge Management Overview	52
6.2	Overview of the TopHat Aligning Approach	55
6.3	Applying Monitoring to Workflow Application	57
6.4	Example Behaviour of Actions at Time Intervals t1-t6	59
7.1	LoM2HiS Evaluation Testbed.	61
7.2	Host Monitor and Communication Model Results.	63
7.3	Run-Time Monitor Results.	64
7.4	Traffic Management Evaluation Testbed.	65

7.5	LoM2HiS Communication Evaluation Result.	66
7.6	Monitoring-Gateway Performance Evaluation Result.	67
7.7	Example of Images for Each of the Three Animations.	69
7.8	Behaviour of Execution Time for Each POV-Ray Application.	70
7.9	Pov-Ray Evaluation Configuration.	71
7.10	POV-Ray Experimentation Results.	72
7.11	Intrusiveness Test Results.	73
7.12	POV-Ray Application Monitoring Cost Relations.	74
7.13	Web Application Evaluation Configuration.	75
7.14	Web Application Cost Relations.	77
7.15	Scheduling Evaluation Testbed.	78
7.16	Scheduling and Deploying With Fixed Resources.	80
7.17	Scheduling and Deploying With On-demand Resource Provisioning Feature.	81
7.18	CASViD Monitor's Intrusion with Different Sampling Frequencies.	87
7.19	Scenario 1 Analyzed Results.	88
7.20	Scenario 2 Analyzed Results.	88
7.21	Scenario 3 Analyzed Results.	89
7.22	Behaviour of Provider Net Utility for the 10-sec Measurement Interval.	90
7.23	Evaluation Testbed	91
7.24	Monitored CPU Utilization	92
7.25	Monitored Memory Utilization	93
7.26	Monitored Storage Utilization	94
7.27	Number of Resource Violations in the Scenarios.	95
7.28	Resource Utilization Levels.	95
7.29	Reconfiguration Actions to Allocate Resources.	96

Selected Publications

The contributions of this thesis is based on work published in scientific conferences, journals, workshops, and books. The following list presents the papers used in the composition of this thesis. Some parts of the papers are included in verbatim. The full list of the author's publication is presented on his home page.

- Vincent C. Emeakaroha, Tiago C. Ferreto, Marco A. S. Netto, Ivona Brandic, Cesar A. F. De Rose. CASViD: Application Level Monitoring for SLA Violation Detection in Clouds. In 36th Annual IEEE Computer and Application International Conference (COMPSAC 2012). Izmir, Turkey, July 16 - 20, 2012.

- Vincent C. Emeakaroha, Marco A. S. Netto, Rodrigo N. Calheiros, Cesar A. F. De Rose. Achieving Flexible SLA and Resource Management in Clouds. Book Chapter in: Achieving Federated and Self-Manageable Cloud Infrastructures: Theory and Practice. Editors: Massimo Villari, Ivona Brandic, and Francesco Tusa. Release Date: May, 2012. IGI Global, 2012, 374 pages.

- Vincent C. Emeakaroha Ivona Brandic, Michael Maurer, Schahram Dustdar. Cloud Resource Provisioning and SLA Enforcement Via LoM2HiS Framework, Concurrency and Computation: Practice and Experience, 2011. To appear.

- Vincent C. Emeakaroha, Michael Maurer, Ivan Breskovic, Ivona Brandic, Schahram Dustdar. SOA and QoS Management for Cloud Computing. Book Chapter in: Cloud Computing: Methodology, System, and Applications. Editors: Lizhe Wang, Rajiv Ranjan, Jinjun Chen, Boualem Benatallah. CRC, Taylor & Francis Group 2011.

- Vincent C. Emeakaroha, Marco A. S. Netto, Rodrigo N. Calheiros, Ivona Brandic, Rajkumar Buyya, Cesar A. F. De Rose. Towards Autonomic Detection of SLA Violations in Cloud Infrastructures. Future Generation Computer Systems, 2011, doi: 10.1016/j.future.-2011.08.018.

- Vincent C. Emeakaroha, Michael Maurer, Ivona Brandic, Schahram Dustdar. FoSII - Foundations of Self-Governing ICT Infrastructures. Special Theme: Cloud Computing Platforms, Software, and Applications. ERCIM News No. 83 (October 2010).

- Vincent C. Emeakaroha, Pawel Labaj, Michael Maurer, Ivona Brandic, David P. Kreil. Optimizing Bioinformatics Workflows for Data Analysis Using Cloud Management Techniques. The 6th Workshop on Workflows in Support of Large-Scale Science (WORKS11), in conjunction with Supercomputing 2011, Seattle, November 12-18, 2011.

- Christoph Stoegerer, Ivona Brandic, Vincent C. Emeakaroha, Wolfgang Kastner, and Thomas Novak. Applying availability SLAs to Traffic Management Systems. IEEE Intelligent Transportation Systems Conference (ITSC 2011) Washington DC, USA - October 5-7, 2011.

- Vincent C. Emeakaroha, Ivona Brandic, Michael Maurer, Ivan Breskovic. SLA-Aware Application Deployment and Resource Allocation in Clouds. The Second IEEE International Workshop on Applied Cloud Computing (CloudApp 2011), in conjunction with the 35th Annual IEEE International Computer Software and Applications Conference (COMPSAC 2011) Munich, Germany, July 18-21 2011.

- Michael Maurer, Ivan Breskovic, Vincent C. Emeakaroha, Ivona Brandic. Revealing the MAPE Loop for the Autonomic Management of Cloud Infrastructures. Workshop on Management of Cloud Systems (MoCS 2011), in association with the IEEE Symposium on Computers and Communications (ISCC 2011), June 28 - July 1 2011, Kerkyra (Corfu) Greece.

- Michael Maurer, Vincent C. Emeakaroha, Ivona Brandic, Joern Altmann. Cost and Benefit of the SLA Mapping Approach for Defining Standardized Goods in Cloud Computing Markets. International Conference on Utility and Cloud Computing (UCC 2010) in conjunction with the International Conference on Advanced Computing (ICoAC 2010), December 14-16, 2010, Chennai, India.

- Vincent C. Emeakaroha, Michael Maurer, Ivona Brandic, Schahram Dustdar. FoSII - Foundations of Self-Governing ICT Infrastructures. Special Theme: Cloud Computing Platforms, Software, and Applications. ERCIM News No. 83 (October 2010).

- Vincent C. Emeakaroha, Marco A. S. Netto, Rodrigo N. Calheiros, Ivona Brandic, and Cesar A. F. De Rose. DeSVi: An Architecture for Detecting SLA Violations in Cloud Computing Infrastructures. 2nd International ICST Conference on Cloud Computing (CloudComp 2010) Barcelona, Spain October 25 - 28, 2010.

- Ivona Brandic, Vincent C. Emeakaroha, Michael Maurer, Sandor Acs, Attila Kertesz, Gabor Kecskemeti, Schahram Dustdar (2010). LAYSI: A Layered Approach for SLA-Violation Propagation in Self-manageable Cloud Infrastructures. The First IEEE International Workshop on Emerging Applications for Cloud Computing (CloudApp 2010), In conjunction with the 34th Annual IEEE International Computer Software and Applications Conference Seoul, Korea, July 19-23 2010.

- Michael Maurer, Ivona Brandic, Vincent C. Emeakaroha, Schahram Dustdar. Towards Knowledge Management in Self-adaptable Clouds. IEEE 2010 Fourth International Workshop of Software Engineering for Adaptive Service-Oriented Systems (SEASS '10), in conjunction with ICWS 2010 and SCC 2010, Miami, Florida, USA, July 5-10, 2010.

- Vincent C. Emeakaroha, Brandic, Ivona, Maurer, Michael, Dustdar, Schahram. Low level Metrics to High level SLAs - LoM2HiS framework: Bridging the gap between monitored metrics and SLA parameters in cloud environments, 2010 International Conference on High Performance Computing and Simulation (HPCS), pp.48-54, June 28 2010-July 2 2010 doi: 10.1109/HPCS.2010.5547150

CHAPTER 1

Introduction

In recent years, and with rapid development of Information Technology (IT), many organizations and enterprises are seeking ways to save operation cost, achieve scalability, good application performance, and high efficiency in resource utilization [167]. With the introduction of compact computing devices such as smart phones and the ubiquitousness of broadband Internet connections, enterprises/customers are focusing on accessing their data and launching applications at any time and from any location [196]. The means of deploying customer application and providing them with enough computational resources to facilitate and guarantee desirable performance has become a challenge.

Many technologies have evolved over the years, such as Distributed Systems, Parallel Computing, Grid, Virtualization, etc. [17, 75, 141, 153, 197] addressing the issues of resource provisioning and application deployment. In today's business requirements, these technologies are less efficient due to their inflexiblity, cost, and lack of scalability. Cloud computing has emerged in the recent time to supplement these technologies and add new features to resource and application provisioning.

There are different definitions and concepts of Cloud computing [43, 176, 201]. However, according to NIST [136], Cloud computing can be defined as a model for enabling convenient on-demand network access to a shared pool of configurable computing resources such as *CPU, networks, storage,* and *memory,* which can be quickly provisioned and released with minimal management effort or Cloud provider assistance.

The fundamental features and characteristics of Cloud computing powering its attractiveness to the consumers are as follows: i) on-demand self-service, ii) rapid elasticity, iii) measured service (pay-as-you-go), iv) ubiquitous network access, and v) resource pooling. These features account for the scalability and cost-effective service provisioning in Cloud environments. There are different delivery and deployment models in Cloud computing. The basic delivery models include the following [20, 113, 126, 140, 158]:

1. **Software as a Service (SaaS)**: In this delivery model, the consumer uses a Cloud application but, he does not control the operating system, hardware, and network devices of the

environment provisioning the application.

2. **Platform as a Service (PaaS)**: Here, a hosting environment is made available to the consumer for their applications. He has the capability of controlling the applications in the host environment. However, the consumer has a limited control of the operating system, hardware, and network devices of the hosting environment.

3. **Infrastructure as a Service (IaaS)**: In this model, the consumer has full access and uses fundamental computing resources such as *CPU, storage, memory, network devices*. The consumer has the ability to control the operating system, hardware, networking infrastructure, and the deployed applications.

The deployment models in Clouds are the different ways of using Cloud infrastructures and services. The following are some of the deployment models [124, 158, 191, 198]:

1. **Public Cloud**: A public Cloud can be described as a means to make services available to all consumers through the Internet. The term 'public' does not necessarily mean that the services are free but they can be fairly inexpensive to use. Furthermore, it does not mean that the consumer's data is publicly visible to others. Public Cloud providers use access control mechanism for their consumers. They offer elastic and cost effective services for application deployment.

2. **Private Cloud**: This deployment model is used by organizations for their private application deployments. It offers many of the features of public Cloud such as elasticity to the organization. The difference to the public Cloud is that access is being granted only to the members of the organization, and there are no restrictions on network bandwidth, security or legal issues. Also in this model, the consumers have greater control of the Cloud infrastructures as in public Cloud.

3. **Hybrid Cloud**: This is a combination of public and private Cloud in different fashions. In this model, organizations can outsource low-risk applications to the public Cloud to save cost or energy.

Having given a brief overview of the Cloud computing technology, we would like to state that the contributions of this thesis are realized in the course of the Foundations of Self-governing ICT Infrastructure (FoSII) research project funded by the Vienna Science and Technology Fund. This project aims to develop an autonomic infrastructure for Cloud management and service level agreement enforcement based on some techniques like monitoring, scheduling, and knowledge management. This thesis concentrates on the monitoring and scheduling challenges in the project. In the next section, we describe these challenges in detail.

1.1 Problem Statement

With the ever growing interest in Cloud computing from both, industry and academia, and the rapid growth of Cloud computational infrastructure resources, the management of the infrastructures to efficiently provision resources and services to customers is now a challenging task.

Cloud management systems consist of components such as, monitoring techniques, scheduling and deployment mechanism, and resource allocation and de-allocation strategies.

The provisioning of services in Clouds is in compliance to a set of predefined non-functional properties specified as Quality of Service (QoS) and negotiated by means of Service Level Agreements (SLAs) [11, 121]. SLA considers obligations, service pricing, and penalties in case of agreement violations. In the Cloud market today, SLAs now form the basis for doing business between the Cloud providers and consumers. Flexible and reliable management of SLA agreements is of paramount importance for both Cloud providers and consumers. On the one hand, prevention of SLA violations avoids costly penalties providers have to pay and on the other hand, based on flexible and timely reactions to possible SLA violations, user interaction with the system can be minimized, which enables Cloud computing to take roots as a flexible and reliable form of on-demand computing.

Furthermore, another important aspect for the usage of SLAs is the required elasticity of Cloud infrastructures. Thus, SLAs are not only used to provide guarantees to end user, they are also used by providers to efficiently manage Cloud infrastructures, considering competing priorities like energy efficiency and attainment of SLA agreements [18, 19] while delivering sufficient elasticity. Moreover, SLAs are also recently used as part of novel Cloud engineering models like Cloud federation [39, 41]. Current monitoring infrastructures lack appropriate solutions for adequate SLA monitoring. The first challenge is to facilitate mapping of measured low-level resource metrics to the form of application based SLA parameters. The second challenge is to determine appropriate monitoring intervals at the application level keeping the balance between the early detection of possible SLA violations and the intrusiveness of the monitoring tools on the whole system.

Although, there is a large body of work considering development of flexible and self-manageable Cloud computing infrastructures [23, 33], there is still a lack of adequate monitoring infrastructures able to predict possible SLA violations. Most of the available monitoring systems rely either on Grid [48, 107, 117, 151] or service-oriented infrastructures [52], which are not directly compatible to Clouds due to the differences in resource usage models, or due to heavily network-oriented monitoring infrastructures [86].

Moreover, to achieve high resource utilization and increased revenue, the providers must be able to schedule resources and deploy different customer applications complying with SLA objectives and, at the same time optimizing the performance of the applications. Currently, there exist numerous work considering scheduling of applications in Clouds [80, 143, 156]. These approaches are usually tailored toward one single SLA objective such as execution time, cost of execution, etc. The design of a generalized scheduling algorithm for optimal mapping of application workload with multiple SLA parameters to resources in Clouds is still an open research issue. In related areas, such algorithms are considered to be NP-hard due to their combinatorial nature [182]. Thus, viable solutions are based on the use of heuristics.

Nevertheless, the idea of scheduling and deploying multiple applications on the same host brings a new set of challenges to the management infrastructure. Each of the applications is being provisioned based on its separate SLA terms. Therefore, the applications have to be monitored separately to enforce the agreed SLA objectives. In this case, carrying out only resource monitoring is not sufficient because at the resource level, one cannot distinguish the resource consumption behaviours of the applications. Thus, there is a need for application-level monitoring techniques. Although some existing research work [21, 77, 106] are considering this issue, there is still a lack of efficient application monitoring tools that are capable to adequately monitor and detect SLA violations of different customer applications.

In addressing these problems, we strive to realize a sophisticated Cloud management infrastructure that is able to schedule, deploy application, and monitor both, at infrastructure-, and application-levels.

1.2 Research Questions

In this section, we concretize the research questions addressed in this thesis. Nevertheless, Section 1.1 has presented the overview of the challenges motivating the research work carried out. Therefore, we concretely address the following questions:

Research Question 1
How can a Cloud provider enforce high-level application SLA objectives based on low-level resource metrics?

The fulfillment of the agreed application SLA objectives, while provisioning in Clouds, depends on the available provider resources in the Cloud environment. In order to determine the resource availability in the Cloud environment, there is a need for an efficient resource monitoring framework. Furthermore, monitoring the low-level resource metrics is not sufficient because of the difference between the low-level resource metrics and the high-level SLA objectives. To resolve these differences, the provider has to map the low-level metrics (*e.g., uptime, downtime*) to an equivalence of the high-level SLA objectives (*e.g., availability*). Thus, adequate monitoring and mapping techniques are necessary.

Research Question 2
How can a Cloud provider determine the optimal measurement interval for cost-efficient monitoring and detection of SLA violations?

With the monitoring of the Cloud infrastructure resources, the provider gains information about the usage of the resources and the current resource availability status. The rate of acquiring this information is an important factor consigning the overall performance of the system and the profit of the provider. On the one hand, monitoring at a high rate delivers fast updates about the resource status to the provider but, it can cause lots of overhead, which eventually degrades the performance of the system. On the other hand, monitoring at a low rate causes the miss of information such as missing to detect SLA violation, which results in paying of SLA penalties by the provider. Therefore, to address this issue, techniques to determine the optimal measurement intervals to efficiently monitor to detect SLA violations are required.

Research Question 3
Are there possibilities to efficiently deploy applications in Clouds, ensure their performance, and thereby achieve high resource utilization?

One of the basic reasons of opting for Cloud solutions by customers is to minimize the cost of maintaining resources and applications locally. Most of the customers are only interested in the execution and performance of their application. These applications have different resource consumption characteristics and, therefore, are not capable of fully utilizing the resources of a virtual machine if deployed alone. In order for the provider to achieve high resource utilization and save the cost of maintaining large number of running virtual machines in the Cloud environment, it is necessary to device a means of scheduling and deploying the applications using minimal number of virtual machine. Furthermore, this scheduling strategy should ensure the performance of the applications based on the agreed SLAs. To the best of our knowledge, none of the existing scheduling algorithms consider multiple SLA objectives in making scheduling decisions.

Research Question 4
How can a Cloud provider manage and guarantee individual SLA objectives of applications executing on the same host?

The guaranteeing of individual customer SLAs for applications being provisioned on the same host is an important management task for the Cloud provider. To achieve this goal, the provider has to monitor the resource consumption behaviour and the performance of each single application differently to ensure that the agreed SLA objectives are not violated. Therefore, the provider requires efficient application-level monitoring techniques for this purpose. The monitoring technique should be capable of automatically determining optimal measurement intervals for the different application monitoring, be less intrusive to the system, and support large scale Cloud environments. None of the existing monitoring framework we studied so far posses these capabilities.

Research Question 5
How can we prevent/correct SLA violation situations in Clouds?

With the monitoring techniques, the Cloud provider can acquire information about the available resources, the application performance status, and predict/detect SLA violation situations. However, he can not prevent or correct the SLA violations. To address this issue, there are needs to integrate knowledge management techniques into the Cloud management infrastructure to provide reactive actions and autonomic behaviours.

1.3 Scientific Contributions

According to the research questions presented in Section 1.2, we highlight in this section the scientific contributions to the state-of-the-art in autonomic Cloud management and SLA enforcement. Our contributions in this thesis have been published in different journals, conferences, workshops, and books. We specify for each contribution, the references where it has been published.

Contribution 1
Low-level resource metrics monitoring and mapping framework

The monitoring of low-level Cloud infrastructure resource metrics and mapping them based on predefined mapping rules to form the equivalence of the high-level SLA parameter objectives are very essential for the management of resources and application provisioning in Clouds. As the core of a Cloud management infrastructure, we designed and implemented the Low-level Metrics to High-level SLA monitoring and mapping (LoM2HiS) framework, which monitors resource metrics and maps the metric values to the equivalence of the high-level SLA parameter objectives in order to guarantee the performance of user applications. Details of this framework are presented in Section 3.1. Contribution 1 has been previously published in [60, 61, 65, 172].

Contribution 2
Architecture for finding optimal measurement intervals for monitoring single application deployment and detecting SLA violations

To efficiently guarantee the Cloud customer applications' performance through monitoring, there is a need for scalable monitoring architecture to detect SLA objective violations. Furthermore, it is important to determine an optimal measurement interval so as not to degrade the system performance with excess monitoring activities or to incur SLA penalties due to missed SLA violation detection. For these purposes, we designed the Detecting SLA Violation Infrastructure (DeSVi) architecture, which consist of components to setup virtual machines, deploy task, and it uses the LoM2HiS framework as a monitoring tool. We present the details of this architecture in Section 3.5. Contribution 2 has been previously published in [62, 66–68].

Contribution 3
SLA-aware application scheduling and deployment mechanism

To further enhance the capability of the Cloud management infrastructure with the ability of scheduling and deploying applications based on multiple SLA terms, we designed and implemented a scheduling heuristic, which integrates a load balancing mechanism to balance the application deployments among the running virtual machines. The scheduling heuristic has the ability to start new virtual machines for further deployments as long as the physical resources in the Cloud environment can accommodate them. The descriptions of this scheduling heuristic is presented in Chapter 4. Contribution 3 has been previously published in [59].

Contribution 4
Application-level monitoring architecture

In order to realize a holistic monitoring technique capable of monitoring at the different layers of Cloud environment and to supplement the Cloud management infrastructure, we designed and implemented an application-level monitoring architecture, which is capable of monitoring the resource consumption behaviours and the performance of each application executing on a shared host. We also implemented an automatic mechanism for determining the optimal measurement intervals for the application monitoring. Details of this application monitoring architecture is presented in Chapter 5. Contribution 4 has been previously published in [63, 130].

Contribution 5
The integration of knowledge management techniques into Cloud management infrastructure

We present in a case study the integration of the knowledge management techniques into the Cloud management infrastructure to achieve autonomic behaviours and to react to detected SLA objective violations. The knowledge management techniques provide reactive actions based on the monitored information. We utilize a scientific workflow application in the case study to demonstrate how to monitor and manage the execution of an application in Clouds. The case study is presented in Section 6.3. Contribution 5 has been previously published in [64].

Contribution 6
The evaluation of the contributions using a real Cloud testbed

We developed a real private Cloud testbed environment for the evaluation of some of the scientific contributions in this thesis. We use different application types to evaluate the designed and implemented framework and architectures. Our developed Cloud testbed is located at the High Performance Computing Lab at Catholic University of Rio Grande do Sul (LAD-PUCRS) Brazil. Chapter 7 presents the different evaluation scenarios and the achieved results respectively. Contribution 6 has been previously published in [60–62, 68].

1.4 Thesis Organization

This thesis is organized as follows:

- Chapter 2 presents some background information on important concepts and about the research project by which course, the work in this thesis is carried out. We first present the Foundations of Self-governing ICT Infrastructure (*FoSII*) research project. After which, we define and describe the concept of service level agreement. We also discuss the concept of autonomic behaviour.

- In Chapter 3, we discuss the Cloud infrastructure monitoring techniques. In particular, we describe the LoM2HiS framework, its design, implementation, and present its application in a traffic management system. Furthermore, we provide details of the design and

7

implementation of the DeSVi architecture, which utilizes the LoM2HiS framework as a monitoring component.

- Chapter 4 describes the SLA-aware application scheduling and deployment heuristic. In the chapter, we first present the motivations for the scheduling approach and describe the basic resource provisioning and deployment models in Clouds. In the next step, we present the design of the scheduling heuristic and the load balancing mechanism after which, we discuss their implementations.

- The Cloud application monitoring architecture is presented in Chapter 5. We discuss the motivation scenario for the development of this monitoring architecture. The design of the architecture and its implementation choices are presented afterwards.

- In Chapter 6, we explain the concept of holistic monitoring and introduce the knowledge management technique, which provides reactive actions to manage resources and avoid SLA violations in a Cloud environment. Furthermore, we present a case study using scientific workflow applications to demonstrate the usage of an autonomic Cloud management infrastructure consisting of the integration of monitoring with knowledge management techniques.

- Chapter 7 presents the evaluations of the achieved framework and architectures in this thesis. It also presents the evaluation of the traffic management system, which utilizes the LoM2HiS framework. For each of the evaluations, we first describe the evaluation testbed configuration and the applications used for the evaluation. Furthermore, we present the evaluation of the case study using bioinformatic workflow application.

- The related work is presented in Chapter 8. We divide the related work into four categories: i) Cloud infrastructure monitoring, ii) Scheduling Mechanism, iii) Cloud Application monitoring, and iv) SLA enforcement and management. We analyze the existing work in each categories and differentiate them to our contributions in this thesis.

- Chapter 9 discusses the conclusion of the work presented in this thesis. We first summarize the work and in the next step, we present the limitations of our proposed solutions. And finally, we describe possible future work arising from the research contributions of this thesis.

CHAPTER 2

Background

This chapter describes some background information on essential concepts necessary for easy understanding of the research work presented in this thesis. We first present the research project by which course, the work in this thesis is carried out in Section 2.1. We discuss the concept of service level agreement in Section 2.2 and finally present some introduction of autonomic behaviour in Section 2.3.

2.1 FoSII Research Project

The acronym FoSII stays for Foundations of Self-governing ICT Infrastructures [74].

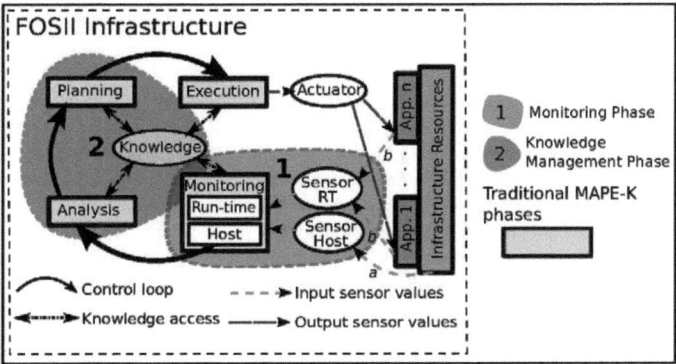

Figure 2.1: FoSII Infrastructure Overview.

This project is funded by the Vienna Science and Technology Fund known in german as Wiener Wissenschafts-, Forschungs und Technologiefonds (WWTF), which fosters solid research on Information Communication Technology (ICT) in Vienna. The FoSII infrastructure proposes models and concepts for autonomic SLA management and enforcement in Clouds. It relies on sophisticated monitoring techniques and advanced knowledge management strategies to achieve these goals.

Figure 2.1 depicts the components of the FoSII infrastructure. It is made up of two core aspects. The first part comprises *the monitoring aspect* and its objective is to provide monitored information to the second part that comprises *the knowledge management aspect*, which analyzes the monitored information and provide reactive actions to manage the Cloud environment. The FoSII infrastructure implements different interfaces such as: (i) application management interface necessary to start the application, upload data, and perform similar management actions and (ii) self-management interface necessary to devise actions in order to prevent SLA violations.

The self-management strategy in FoSII, as shown in Figure 2.1, consist of sensors for detecting changes in the desired state and for reacting to those changes [23]. The host monitor sensors continuously monitor the infrastructure resource metrics (input sensor values arrow a in Figure 2.1) and provide the autonomic manager with the current resource status. The run-time monitor sensors sense future SLA violation threats (input sensor values arrow b in Figure 2.1) based on resource usage experiences and predefined threat thresholds. These monitored information are passed to the knowledge management for further processing.

The knowledge management receives the monitored information in the analysis phase and analyzes it to determine the resource allocation or preventive action to take. In the planning phase, the selected action is scheduled for execution considering the timing of the execution and strategies to avoid oscillation in applying the actions. The execution phase carries out the execution of the proposed actions on the Cloud environment with the help of actuators. The whole process executes continuously to efficiently manage the Cloud infrastructure and the application SLA objectives. The knowledge management aspect in FoSII is based on knowledge databases for its operations. Currently, we are investigating different knowledge database techniques such as Case Based Reasoning (CBR) [131, 132] and rule-base approaches [133] for this purpose. Here, we present an overview of our research work on CBR.

Case-Based Reasoning was first built on top of FreeCBR [76], but is now a completely independent Java framework taking into account, however, basic ideas of FreeCBR. It can be defined as the process of solving problems based on past experiences [1]. In more detail, it tries to solve a *case*, which is a formatted instance of a problem by looking for similar cases from the past and reusing the solutions of these cases to solve the current one.

Figure 2.2 presents an overview of the CBR process. The ideas of using CBR in SLA management are to have rules stored in a database that engage the CBR system once a threshold value has been reach for a specific SLA parameter. The notification information are fed into the CBR system as new cases by the monitoring component. Then, CBR prepared with some initial meaningful cases stored in DB2 (Figure 2.2), chooses the set of cases, which are most similar to the new case based on various factors as described in [132]. From these cases, we select the one with the highest utility measured previously and trigger its corresponding action as the proposed

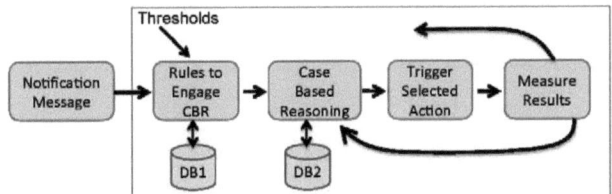

Figure 2.2: Case-Based Reasoning Process Overview

action to solve the new case. Finally, we measure in a later time interval the result of this action in comparison to the initial case and store it with its calculated utilities as a new case in the CBR. Doing this, we can constantly learn new cases and evaluate the usefulness of our triggered actions [61].

```
1.  (
2.    (App,   1),
3.    (
4.    ((Incoming Bandwidth, 12.0),
5.     (Outgoing Bandwidth, 20.0),
6.     (Storage, 1200),
7.     (Availability, 99.5),
8.     (Running on PMs, 1)),
9.     (Physical Machines, 20)
10.   ),
11.   "Increase Incoming Bandwidth share by 5%",
12.   (
13.    ((Incoming Bandwidth, 12.6),
14.     (Outgoing Bandwidth, 20.1),
15.     (Storage, 1198),
16.     (Availability, 99.5),
17.     (Running on PMs, 1)),
18.     (Physical Machines, 20)
19.   ),
20.   0.002
21.  )
```

Figure 2.3: Case Based-Reasoning Example.

In general, a typical CBR cycle consists of the following phases assuming that a new case was just received:

1. Retrieve the most similar case or cases to the new one.

2. Reuse the information and knowledge in the similar case(s) to solve the problem.

3. Revise the proposed solution.

4. Retain the parts of this experience likely to be useful for future problem solving. (Store new case and corresponding solution into knowledge database.)

Furthermore, we present here a practical demonstration of a CBR system, showing the management of SLA objectives as depicted in Figure 2.3. A complete case consists of (a) the ID of application being provisioned (line 2, Figure 2.3); (b) the initial case measured by the monitoring component and mapped to the SLAs including the application SLA parameter values and global Cloud information like number of running virtual machines (lines 4-9); (c) the executed action (line 11); (d) the resulting case measured some time interval later (lines 13-18) as in (b); and (e) the resulting utility (line 20). We discuss more about knowledge management in Section 6.2. However, Knowledge management is not the focus of this thesis. Full details on this topic can be found in [131–133].

The work carried out in this thesis concentrates on the monitoring aspect of the FoSII infrastructure. We show in Chapter 6 using a case study how the monitoring and the knowledge management aspects are integrated together to realize an autonomic Cloud management infrastructure.

2.2 Service Level Agreement

Service Level Agreement (SLA) is a term widely used in the telecommunication and networking area to specify Quality of Service (QoS) objectives [42, 46, 148, 168, 188]. It is now adopted in the field of computer science to serve the same purpose of specifying quality of service for Internet offered services. In Cloud computing, services and resources are provisioned through the Internet. Thus, SLA forms the basis for managing the business aspect of Cloud computing technology [28–30].

Table 2.1: SLA Agreement Example.

SLA Parameter	SLA Objective
Availability	$\geq 99\,\%$
Response Time	> 5 ms
Storage	> 100 GB
Memory	> 3 GB
Network Bandwidth	> 100 Mbit/s

A service level agreement can be defined as a contract signed between a Cloud provider and a customer describing functional and non-functional characteristics of a service including QoS requirements, penalties in case of violations, and a set of metrics, which are used to measure the provisioning of the requirements [53, 111, 144]. The goal of an SLA parameter is described as its objective popularly known as Service Level Objective (SLO). Table 2.1 presents an example of SLA agreement specifying some objectives in Clouds.

The management of SLAs [163, 185] is made up of different aspects such as i) SLA specification, ii) SLA negotiation, iii) SLA monitoring, and iv) SLA enforcement. SLA specification details the strategy and processes of specifying the agreement terms in a specific format. There are many existing work in this area such as [22, 51, 57, 127]. The negotiation of SLA deals with the technique of setting up the agreement between the provider and the customer. There are lots of effort going on in this area to address this issue like [25, 146, 190, 195, 202]. The areas of SLA specifications and negotiations are not the focus of this work. In this thesis, we focus on developing techniques and mechanisms for SLA monitoring and enforcement. We describe in Chapters 3 and 5 our approach for SLA monitoring to detect violation situations at the different Cloud layers.

2.3 Autonomic Behaviour

Autonomic behaviour is characterised by capabilities such as self-configuration, self-diagnosing, and self-healing, focusing at allowing the system to manage failures of its components and to facilitate continuous functioning in the presence of errors. Autonomic behaviour is a concept derived from autonomic computing [9, 119], which aims to provide means of automatical management of computing resources [89, 122]. Autonomic computing is inspired by the functions of the human nervous system and is aimed at designing and building systems that are self-managing. Autonomic systems are being adopted for self-management of complex large scale distributed system that have become manually unmanageable [7, 47, 54].

In autonomic systems, humans do not control the system. Moreover, they define the general policies and rules that serve as input for the self-management process. Such systems constantly adapt themselves to changing environmental conditions like workload, hardware, and software failures [99, 105]. Nowadays, the concepts of autonomic system are being applied in all aspects of sciences to provide intelligent decision making, and to realize automations relieving humans from routine or complicated tasks.

An important characteristic of an autonomic system is an intelligent closed loop of control where an autonomic manager manages the elements' states and behaviours. Typically, control loops are implemented following MAPE (Monitoring, Analysis, Planning, and Execution) steps [23, 134]. The control loop with its components and the Knowledge database makes the autonomic manager to be self-manageable. The managed resources can be software or hardware resources that are given autonomic behaviour in accordance with an autonomic manager. Thus, the managed resources can be operating systems, wired or wireless network, CPU, database, servers, routers, application modules, Web services or virtual machines, etc [199].

Autonomic computing is to promote self-manageable goals of various components in a whole system. Autonomic computing system involves service-oriented technology, agent technology, adaptive control theory, machine learning, optimization theory, and many more [70, 103, 199]. The aim of introducing this concept in this thesis is to achieve autonomic behaviour in our proposed Cloud management infrastructure, whereby appropriate actions are taken, based on the monitored information to prevent/correct SLA violation situations, and to allocate or de-allocate resources to achieve high resource utilizations and avoid resource wastage. We demonstrated in Chapter 6 the usage of this concept.

CHAPTER 3

Cloud Infrastructure Monitoring

Cloud computing promises on-demand and scalable resource provisioning to its customers based on pre-agreed service level agreement objectives. The management of Cloud resources and the guaranteeing of the SLA objectives are challenging. In this chapter, we present the Cloud infrastructure monitoring techniques, which are the basis for the Cloud management infrastructure. We first discuss the metrics monitoring and mapping framework, after which we describe the usage of this framework in a traffic management system. Towards the end of the chapter, we present the DeSVi architecture.

3.1 Metrics Monitoring and Mapping Motivation

In order to guarantee an agreed SLA in Clouds, the Cloud provider must be capable of monitoring its infrastructure (host) resource metrics to enforce the agreed service level objectives. However, most of the existing monitoring technologies are designed for Grid environments [48, 151], which makes their usage in Clouds inappropriate due to the differences in resource usage models. In Grids [107], resources are mostly owned by different individuals/enterprises, and in some cases, as desktop Grids for instance, resources are only available for usage when the owners are not using them [117]. Therefore, resource availability varies much and this impacts its usage for application provisioning, whereas in Cloud computing, resources are owned by an enterprise (Cloud provider), provisioning them to customers in a pay-as-you-go manner. Therefore, availability of resources is more stable and resources can be provisioned on-demand. Hence, the monitoring strategies used for detection of SLA violations in Grids cannot be directly applied to Clouds.

This problem motivates the development of the Low-level Metric to High-level SLA (LoM2HiS) monitoring and mapping framework to address the challenges in enforcing the agreed SLA objectives and managing resources in Clouds. These challenges can be described using a use case scenario presented in the next section.

Use Case Scenario

The essence of using SLA in Cloud business is to guarantee customers a certain level of quality for their services. In a situation where this level of quality is not met, the provider pays penalties for the breach of contract. Figure 3.1 presents the use case motivation scenario. In a Cloud environment, services and applications are being executed on the physical and virtual resources. However, the quality of service objective to determine the performance of the application is described as a high-level SLA parameter for example *availability, throughput, etc*. But, the applications are running on physical or virtual resources, which are characterized with low-level metrics such as *CPU, memory, uptime, downtime, etc*.

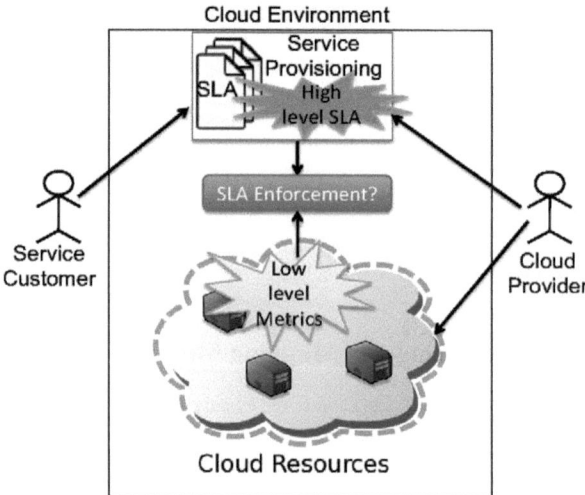

Figure 3.1: LoM2HiS Motivation Scenario.

Thus, there is a gap between the low-level resource metrics and the high-level SLA parameters. To cover this gap and enforce the agreed SLA terms, we propose and develop the LoM2HiS framework. We present the conceptual design of the framework including the run-time and host monitors, and the SLA mapping database. We discuss our novel communication model based on queuing networks ensuring the scalability of the LoM2HiS framework. Moreover, we demonstrate sample mappings from the low-level resource metrics to the high-level SLA parameters. The *LoM2HiS* framework represents a major step towards achieving the goals of the FoSII infrastructure project [74].

3.2 LoM2HiS Design Details

In this section, we give the details of the LoM2HiS framework [60, 61] and describe its components and their designs.

Framework Overview

In this framework, we assumed that the SLA negotiation process is completed and the agreed SLAs are stored in the repository for service provisioning. Beside the SLAs, the predefined threat thresholds are also stored in a repository. The concept of detecting future SLA violation threats is designed by defining more restrictive thresholds known as threat thresholds that are stricter than the normal SLA objective violation thresholds. For this framework, we assume predefined threat thresholds.

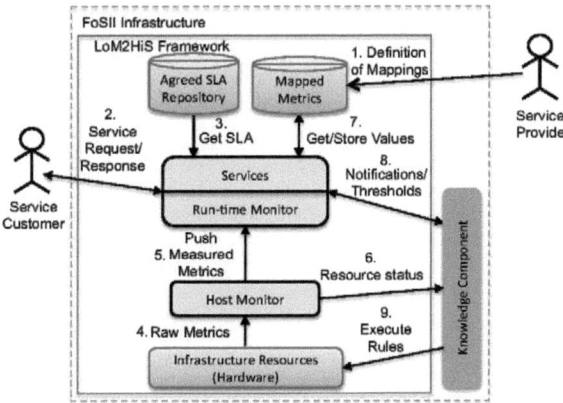

Figure 3.2: LoM2HiS Framework Overview.

Figure 3.2 presents the architecture of our LoM2HiS framework. The service component including the run-time monitor represents the application layer where services are deployed using a Web Service container e.g., Apache Axis. The run-time monitor is designed to monitor the services based on the negotiated and agreed SLAs. After agreeing on SLA terms, the service provider creates mapping rules for the LoM2HiS mappings (step 1 in Figure 3.2) using Domain Specific Languages (DSLs). DSLs are small languages that can be tailored to a specific problem domain. Once the customer requests the provisioning of an agreed service (step 2), the run-time monitor loads the service SLA from the agreed SLA repository (step 3). Service provisioning is based on the infrastructure resources, which represent the hosts and network resources in a data centre for hosting Cloud services. The resource metrics are measured by monitoring agents, and the measured raw metrics are accessed by the host monitor (step 4). The host monitor extracts metric-value pairs from the raw metrics and transmits them periodically to the run-time monitor (step 5) and to the knowledge component (step 6) using our designed communication model.

Upon receiving the measured metrics, the run-time monitor maps the low-level metrics based on predefined mapping rules to form the equivalence of the agreed SLA objectives. The mapping results are stored in the mapped metric repository (step 7), which also contains the predefined mapping rules. The run-time monitor uses the mapped values to monitor the status of the deployed services. In case future SLA violation threats occur, it notifies (step 8) the knowledge component for preventive actions. The knowledge component also receives the predefined threat thresholds (step 8) for possible adjustments due to environmental changes at run-time. This component works out appropriate preventive actions to avert future SLA violation threats based on the resource status (step 6) and defined rules. The knowledge component's decisions (e.g., assign more CPU to a virtual host) are executed on the infrastructure resources (step 9).

The LoM2HiS framework is designed to be scalable. In its design, the separation of the host monitor and the run-time monitor makes it possible to deploy these two components on different hosts. This decision is focused toward increasing the scalability of the framework and facilitating its usage in distributed and parallel environments.

Host Monitor

This section describes the host monitor component, which is located at the Cloud infrastructure resource level. We explain its design strategy and later present the implementation details.

The host monitor is responsible for processing monitored values delivered by the monitoring agents embedded in the infrastructure resources. The monitoring agents are capable of measuring both hardware and network resources. Figure 3.3 presents the host monitoring system.

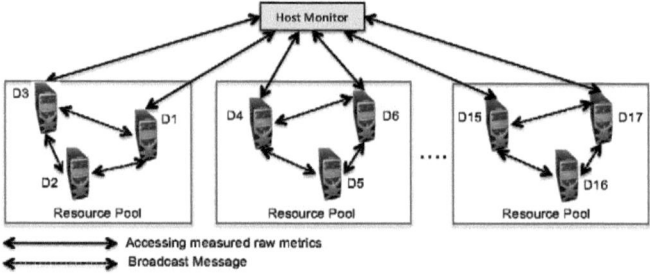

Figure 3.3: Host Monitoring System

As shown in Figure 3.3, the monitoring agent embedded in Device 1 (D1) measures its resource metrics and broadcasts them to D2 and D3. Equally, the monitoring agent in D2 measures and broadcasts its measured metrics to D1 and D3. Thus, we achieve a replica management system in the sense that each device has a complete result of the monitored infrastructure. The host monitor can access these results from any device. It can be configured to access different devices at the same time for monitored values. In case one fails, the result would be accessed from the others. This eradicates the problem of a bottleneck system and offers fault-tolerant capabilities. Note that a device can be a physical machine, a virtual machine, a storage device, or a network device. Furthermore, it should be noted that the above described broadcasting mechanism is configurable and can be deactivated in a Cloud environment where there are lots of devices within the resource pools to avoid communication overheads, which may consequently lead to degraded overall system performance.

The decision to separate the monitoring agents from the data processing units aims to make this framework scalable and less intrusive. Processing the monitored data in a separate node frees the resources on the computing nodes for computational tasks thereby reducing the monitoring effects on these node to a minimum and allowing the computational tasks achieve high performance.

Run-Time Monitor

The run-time monitor component is an integral part of the application deployment mechanism. In this section, we present the detailed description of this component.

The run-time monitor carries out the low-level metrics to high-level SLA mappings. Thus, based on the mapped values, the SLA objectives, and the predefined thresholds, it continuously monitors the customer application status and performance. Its operations are based on three information sources: (i) the resource metric-value pairs received from the host monitor; (ii) the SLA parameter objective values stored in the agreed SLA database; and (iii) the predefined threat threshold values. The metric-value pairs are low-level entities and the SLA objective values are high-level entities, so for the run-time monitor to work with these two values, they must be mapped into common values.

Mapping of low-level metrics to high-level SLAs: As discussed previously, the run-time monitor chooses the mapping rules to apply based on the application being provisioned. That is, for each application type, there is a set of defined rules for performing their SLA parameter mappings. These rules are used to compose, aggregate, or convert the low-level metrics to form the high-level SLA parameter. We distinguish between simple and complex mapping rules. A simple mapping rule maps one-to-one from low-level to high-level, as for example mapping low-level metric *disk space* to high-level SLA parameter *storage*. In this case, only the units of the quantities are considered in the mapping rule. Complex mapping rules consist of predefined formulae for the calculation of specific SLA parameters using the resource metrics. For the evaluations in Section 7.1, we execute simple mapping rules. Nevertheless, Table 3.1 presents some complex mapping rules.

In the mapping rules presented in Table 3.1, the downtime variable represents the *mean time to repair (MTTR)*, which denotes the time it takes to bring a system back online after a failure situation and the uptime represents the *mean time between failure (MTBF)*, which denotes the time the system was operational between the last system failure to the next. The unit of the availability equation is in percentage. In this equation, we assume that the *uptime* and *downtime* variables are greater than or equal to zero. R_{in} is the response time for sending a request in the inwards communication direction and is calculated as $\frac{packetsize}{bandwidthin-inbytes}$ in seconds. The *packetsize* is the size of the query sent in and its unit is in megabit. The *bandwidthin* is the total

Table 3.1: Complex Mapping Rules.

Resource Metrics	SLA Parameter	Mapping Rule
downtime, uptime	Availability (A)	$A = \left(1 - \frac{downtime}{uptime+downtime}\right) * 100$
inbyte, outbytes, packetsize, bandwidthin, bandwidthout	Response Time (R_{total})	$R_{total} = R_{in}(s) + R_{out}(s)$

bandwidth for communicating in the inwards direction and its unit is in megabit per second. The *inbytes* is the amount of bandwidth already in use on this channel and its unit is in megabit per second. R_{out} is the response time for receiving an answer in the outwards communication directions and is calculated as $\frac{packetsize}{bandwidthout-outbytes}$ in seconds. The meaning of the variables in this equation are similar to those in the R_{in} equation and their units are the same. The response time equation shown in Table 3.1 considers only the data transfer time values. It does not include computational time values because in our experiments with web applications, these values are small and negligible. Therefore, our response time equation is custom to web application and does not represent a generalized formula for other application types. The mapped SLAs are stored in the mapped metric database for usage during the monitoring phase.

Monitoring SLA objectives and notifying the knowledge component: In this phase, the run-time monitor accesses the mapped metrics' database to get the mapped SLA parameter values that are equivalent to the agreed SLA objectives, which it uses together with the predefined thresholds in the monitoring process to detect future SLA violation threats or real SLA violation situation. This is achieved by comparing the mapped SLA values against the threat thresholds to detect future violation threats and against SLA objective thresholds to detect real violation situations. In case of detection, it dispatches notification messages to the knowledge component to avert the threats or correct the violation situation. An example of SLA violation threat is something like an indication that the system is running out of storage. In such a case the knowledge component acts to increase the system storage. Real violations occur only if the system is unable to resolve the cause of a violation threat notification. In such a case, appropriate data are logged for calculating the amount of penalty the provider pays for the violations.

3.3 LoM2HiS Implementation Choices

The LoM2HiS framework implementation targets the fulfilment of some fundamental Cloud requirements such as scalability, efficiency, and reliability. To achieve these aims, the framework is based on well-established and tested open source projects.

Host Monitor Implementation

The host monitor implementation uses the GMOND module from the GANGLIA open source project [129] as the monitoring agent. The GMOND module is a standalone component of the

GANGLIA project. The monitoring agents are embedded in each of the computing nodes and we use them to monitor the resource metrics of these nodes. The monitored results are presented in an XML file and written to a predefined network socket. We implemented a Java routine to listen to this network socket where the GMOND writes the XML file containing the monitored metrics to access the file for processing.

The processing of the monitored data is carried out in a separate host. For this purpose, we implemented an XML parser using the well-known open source SAX API [159] to parse the XML file to extract the metric-value pairs. The measured metric-value pairs are sent to the run-time monitor using our implemented communication mechanism. These processes can be done once or repeated periodically depending on the monitoring strategy being used.

Communication Mechanism

The components of a Cloud management infrastructure exchange large numbers of messages with each other, and within the components. Thus, there is a need for a reliable and scalable means of communication.

To satisfy this need of communication means, we designed and implemented a communication mechanism based on the Java Message Service (JMS) API, which is a Java Message Oriented Middleware (MOM) API for sending messages between two or more clients [97]. In order to use a JMS, there is a need for a JMS provider that is capable of managing the sessions and the queues. In this case, we use the well-established open source Apache ActiveMQ [3] for this purpose.

The implemented communication model is a sort of queuing network. It realizes an inter-process communication for passing messages within the Cloud management infrastructure and between the components of the LoM2HiS framework, due to the fact that the components can run on different machines at different locations. This queue makes the communication mechanism highly efficient and scalable.

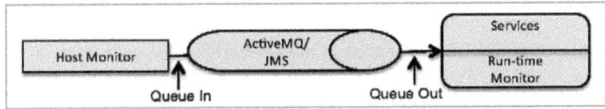

Figure 3.4: Communication Mechanism Overview

Figure 3.4 presents an example scenario expressing the usage of the communication mechanism in the LoM2HiS framework. The scenario of Figure 3.4 depicts the processes of extracting the low-level metrics from the monitoring agents embedded in the computing nodes, processing the gathered information in the host monitor, and passing the derived metric-value pairs to the run-time monitor for mapping and SLA objective monitoring.

Run-Time Monitor Implementations

The run-time monitor receives the measured metric-value pairs and passes them into the Esper engine for further processing. Esper is a component of Complex Event Processing (CEP) and Event Stream Processing (ESP) applications, available for Java as Esper, and for .NET as NEsper [69]. CEP is a technology to process events and discover complex patterns among multiple streams of event data while ESP deals with the task of processing multiple streams of event data with the goal of identifying the meaningful events within those streams, and deriving meaningful information from them.

We apply Esper because the JMS system used in our communication model is stateless and as such makes it hard to deal with temporal data and real-time queries. From the Esper engine the metric-value pairs are delivered as events each time their values change between measurements. This strategy reduces drastically the number of events/messages processed in the run-time monitor. We use an XML parser to extract the SLA parameters and their corresponding objective values from the SLA document and store them in a database. The LoM2HiS mappings are realized in Java methods and the returned mapped SLA objectives are stored in the mapped metrics database.

For data management, we introduce MySQL database in this framework for storing and querying information. We use Hibernate to realize an interface between the run-time monitor classes and MySQL database. Hibernate is a high-performance Object/Relational persistence and query service. The most flexible and powerful Object/Relational solution on the market. Hibernate takes care of mapping from Java classes to database tables and from Java data types to SQL data types. It provides data query and retrieval facilities that significantly reduce development time [91]. With this database, the Cloud provider now has the capability to create a graphical interface for displaying the monitored metric values and the SLA objective status including the reported violation threats and real violation situations.

The performance evaluation of the LoM2HiS framework and the explanation of the achieved results are presented in Section 7.1.

3.4 Applying LoM2HiS to Traffic Management Systems

In this section, we present the application of the LoM2HiS framework in a traffic management system as done in [172]. We first discuss background details of the traffic management system and it challenges after which, we describe the integration of the monitoring framework into this system.

TMS Background

Traffic Management Systems (TMS) are manifold in terms of complexity and functionality but share the common objective of information retrieval from the field (through detectors like inductive loops) as well as information propagation to the traffic participant (through actuators such as Variable Message Signs (VMS)). They consist of numerous subsystems built up in a hierarchical structure of components (e.g., sensors, actuators, outstations, or routers). Depending on the system's aim, it incorporates different levels of control [81] ranging from fixed time operation to smart control strategies.

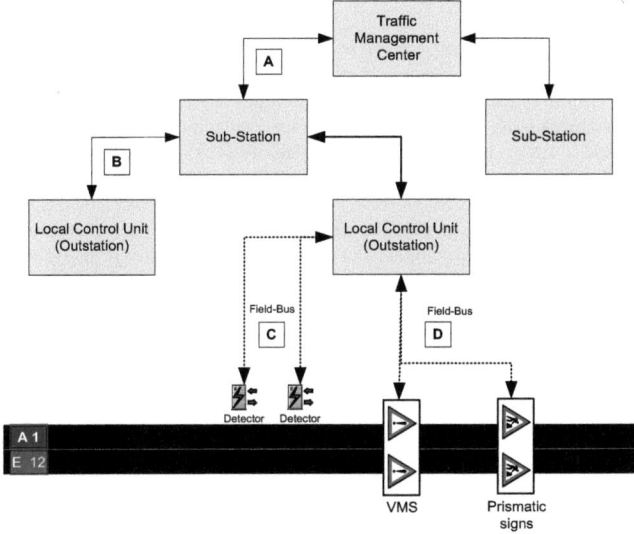

Figure 3.5: Components of a Traffic Management System.

As shown in Figure 3.5, which is gotten from [172], at the highest level of the TMS, a *Traffic Management Center (TMC)* collects data from *Sub-Stations (SS)* and forwards the information to its users for global strategies concerning road traffic monitoring and control. The SS collects intermediate data for controlling particular motorway lines via actuators using the collected data. Furthermore, the SS aggregates the data of specific areas and sent it to the TMC [104]. Nevertheless it also gathers environmental data.

The SS are interconnected to one or more *Local Control Units (LCU)* that are in turn wired to *sensors* (e.g., loop detectors, radar detectors) and *actuators* (e.g., gates, traffic lights, VMS). They are responsible for data processing and autonomous control tasks. Several detection- and/or actuation-sites may be assigned to an LCU. The minimum system configuration of a TMS can be composed of an autonomously acting LCU controlling a single VMS. The maximum system configuration may consist of multiple levels of control and monitoring facilities, where each level is designed for autonomous operation as a kind of fallback in case of breakdown of a higher order level facility [171].

As discussed in [170], communication facilities differ throughout the hierarchical structure of the TMS depending on the levels involved. Different regions are restricted (but de-facto) standards are dedicated to specific communication levels (e.g., A – D in Figure 3.5), which is similar to the approach in [110]. We assume that the levels A and B support IP-based communication whilst levels C and D may use field-bus based master-slave communication. In the remainder of this work, we assume TLS 2002 [79] as the appropriate protocol for communication on the field-bus level.

Today system operators often demand for a certain availability of the TMS. For this reason, maintenance contractors and component vendors need to provide guarantee for a certain availability of the overall system and its components to fulfill the requirements. As shown in Figure 3.5, the overall availability of a TMS depends on the availability of each node in the system. In order to be able to automatically enforce the availability SLA objectives, the required low-level metrics need to be monitored for every node on each level of control in the system architecture. This means the components of the system must be instrumented for feeding back these metrics that can then be mapped to high-level application specific SLA-parameters. As different communication technologies might be involved, the assumption of IP-based communication throughout all levels of hierarchy (as made for Cloud Environments in [60]), is not applicable. Therefore, like the monitoring agents for IP-based nodes, *monitoring gateways* are needed to bridge the gap to non IP-based nodes in the TMS.

LoM2HiS for TMS-Infrastructures

In this section, we describe the application of the LoM2HiS framework to the TMS-Infrastructures. We describe the process of extending and integrating the monitoring components in the traffic management system.

Applying the LoM2HiS Framework to TMS

As described in Section 3.2, the LoM2HiS framework consists of some components like: the *Host Monitor* gathering information from the deployed monitoring agents and the *Run-time Monitor* that processes information and performs SLA enforcement.

As shown in Figure 3.5, communication facilities differs among the hierarchy levels. The monitoring agents can not be directly applied to the nodes at each level. Thus, in Figure 3.5, levels A and B support IP-based communication while levels C and D use field-bus based communication. Therefore, only nodes above levels C and D can be supervised using monitoring agents.

The nodes on the field-level can be observed by extending the LCU operation with the help of a monitoring gateway. The monitoring gateway functions as the LCU's monitoring agent as well as a proxy for the nodes, which includes sensors and actuators connected to it. These slave-nodes are distinguished by adding an additional unique digit (e.g., 1.0.0.1.**1**) to the IP of the master-node (1.0.0.1). Figure 3.6 shows the application of the LoM2HiS framework.

There are different means of deriving the important metrics indicating the liveliness of a specific node from the field-bus communication, which include the following: i) *Physical check* of communication (i.e., the response of the node to (OSI-2) requests), ii) *Syntactical check* of communication (i.e., interpretation of the protocol-specific data (OSI-7) exchanged over the field-bus), and iii) *Semantical check* of communication (e.g., *throughput* by the means of the

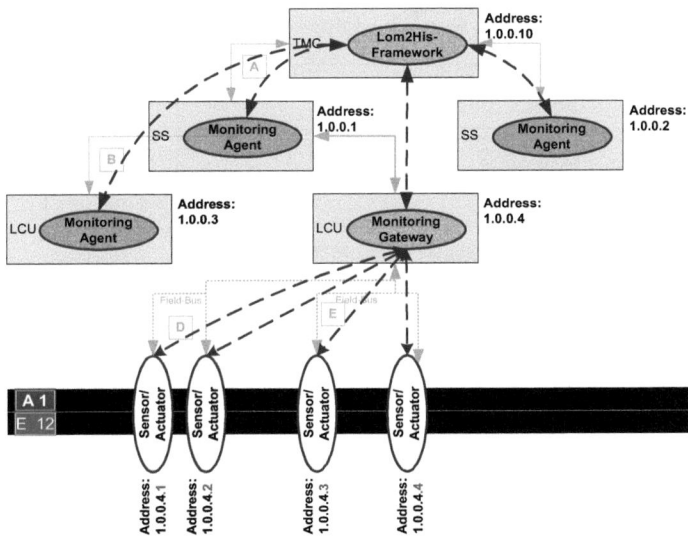

Figure 3.6: Applying LoM2HiS to TMS.

number of PDU's sent and received per unit of time, *response-rate* by the means of the number of correct responses on requests).

By applying monitoring agents to IP-based nodes and covering non IP-based nodes by custom monitoring gateways, the traffic management system is prepared for delivering the low-level metrics required for SLA enforcement.

As mentioned earlier, the host monitor processes monitored values delivered by the monitoring agents and the monitoring gateways embedded in the nodes of the TMS. It extracts the metric-value pairs from the raw metrics and transmits them *periodically* to the Run-time Monitor. The Run-time Monitor chooses the mapping rules to apply based on the type of service being provisioned. The mapping rules are used to compose, aggregate, or convert the low-level metrics to form the equivalence of the high-level SLA parameters.

The whole information flow from the sensor/actuator nodes up to the LoM2HiS framework is shown in Figure 3.7. The Host-Monitor transmits its data periodically (e.g., every 30 seconds) to the Run-time Monitor. The Run-time Monitor in turn inserts the metrics with the actual timestamp into the database. We utilize these characteristics in the following assumptions:

1. timestamps for the raw metrics on the Sensor/Actuator or monitoring gateway level respectively may be omitted since the host monitor assures a database-entry every specified interval of time,

25

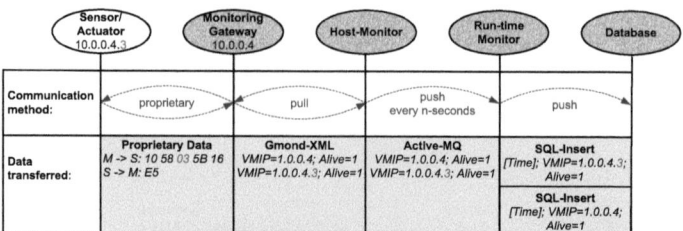

Figure 3.7: LoM2HiS Dataflow.

2. for each node, we calculate the uptime by multiplying the number of entries indicating "alive" in each interval of time,

3. for each node, we calculate the downtime by multiplying the number of entries not indicating "alive" in each interval of time.

The uptime and downtime metrics are represented by *views* stored in the database. These views are designed as complex mapping rules for example to derive the high-level SLA-parameter "Availability" as shown in Table 3.1. In the mapping rule, the downtime variable represents the mean time to repair and the uptime represents the mean time between failures.

Through the application of these changes to the framework, we extended the run-time monitor from monitoring services to monitoring of nodes, which is the core requirement to guarantee high availability in traffic management systems.

We present in Section 7.2 some evaluations of the adoption of LoM2HiS framework in traffic management system. We show the scalability of the monitoring framework and discuss the achieved result.

3.5 DeSVi Architecture Motivation

The importance of efficient SLA violation detection for both Cloud providers and consumers cannot be over emphasized. Currently, there are some existing body of work considering the development of flexible management infrastructures for large-scale systems [33], nevertheless, there is a lack of adequate monitoring infrastructure to detect possible SLA violations. Moreover, the available infrastructures are not capable of setting up virtual machines in Clouds and deploying customer tasks.

Furthermore, the determination of optimal measurement intervals for monitoring the low-level metrics is still an open research issue. Too frequent measurement intervals may negatively affect the overall system performance, whereas too infrequent measurement intervals may cause heavy SLA violations.

The DeSVi architecture [62, 68] aims to address these challenges of efficiency in monitoring resources and detecting application SLA violations in Clouds. The architecture utilizes the

LoM2HiS framework for resource monitoring and low-level metrics mapping. In the next section, we present a motivating use case scenario for the development of this architecture.

Motivating Use Case Scenario

This use case scenario describes the essence of the DeSVi architecture. In this use case and the setup for DeSVi, we assume the deployment of one application per virtual or physical machine. Figure 3.8 presents the motivating scenario.

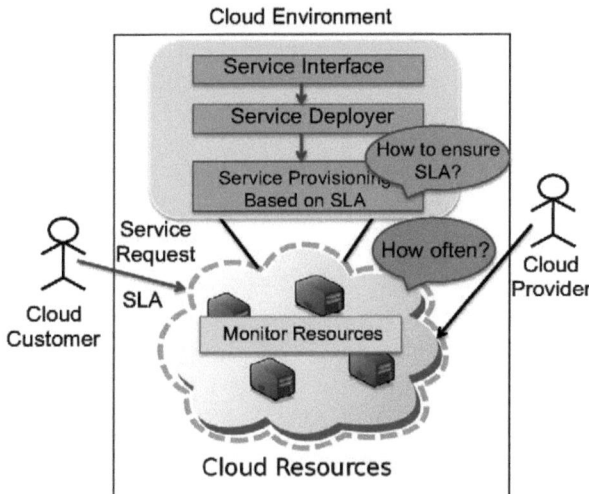

Figure 3.8: DeSVi Motivating Scenario.

As previous explained, Cloud providers can enforce application SLA objectives by monitoring the resource metrics and mapping them to the equivalence of the high-level SLA parameters. However, the questions now are how often should the providers monitor? And how can they determine the optimal measurement intervals in order to achieve efficiency in monitoring? Because monitoring at high rate causes overheads, which degrades the overall system performance and at the same time, monitoring at low rate risks missing the detection of SLA violations.

To address this question, we propose and develop the DeSVi architecture, which consists of different components for the deployment and management of application provisioning.

27

3.6 DeSVi Design Details

This section describes in detail the Detecting SLA Violation infrastructure–*DeSVi architecture*, its components, and how the components interact with one another (Figure 3.9). The proposed architecture is designed to handle the complete service provisioning management lifecycle in Cloud environments. The service provisioning lifecycle includes activities such as service deployment, resource allocation to tasks, resource monitoring, and SLA violation detection.

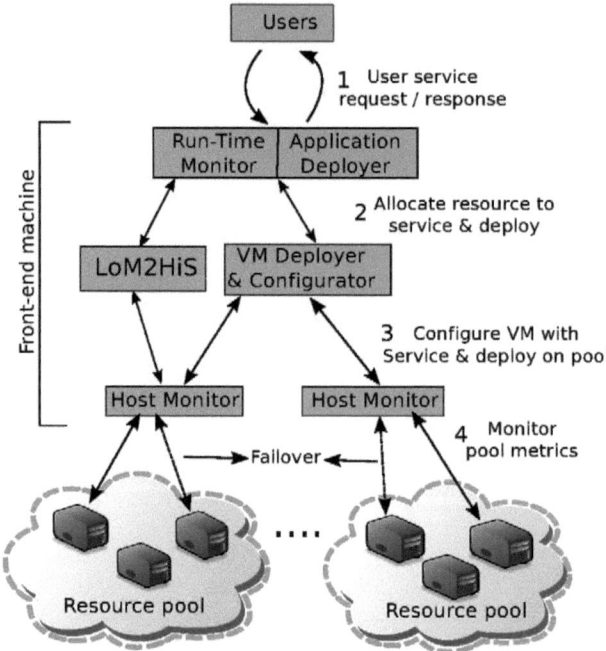

Figure 3.9: Overview of the DeSVi Architecture and Component's Interaction.

The topmost layer represents the users (customers) who place service provisioning requests through a defined application interface (step 1 in Figure 3.9) to the Cloud provider. The provider handles the user service requests based on the negotiated and agreed SLAs with the users. The application deployer, which is located on the same layer as the run-time monitor, allocates necessary Virtual Machine (VM) resources for the requested service and arranges its deployment on the Cloud environment (step 2). The deployment of VMs and environmental configurations are performed by the AEF (Automated Emulation Framework) [33] (step 3). The host monitor observes the metrics of the resource pool comprising virtual machines and physical hosts (step 4). The mapping between the resource metrics (monitored by the host monitor) and SLAs (monitored by the run-time monitor) is managed by the LoM2HiS framework.

The arrow termed *Failover* as presented in Figure 3.9 indicates redundancy in the monitoring mechanism. The host monitor is designed to use monitoring agents as mentioned in Section 3.2, which are embedded in each node in the resource pool to monitor the metrics of the node. Such monitoring agents broadcast their monitored values to the other agents in the same resource pool, creating the possibility of accessing the whole resource pool status from any node in the pool. The metric broadcasting mechanism is configurable and can be deactivated if necessary but it can obviate the problem of a bottleneck master node for accessing the monitored metrics of the resource pool.

The DeSVi architecture is designed to monitor and detect SLA violation in a single Cloud data center. To be able to manage a Cloud environment with multiple data centers, we intend to apply a decentralization approach where the proposed system would be installed on each data center. The LoM2HiS component in our system is already designed with a scalable communication mechanism, which can be easily utilized to allow communication between data centers. In the following sections we explain all components of our system in detail.

Application Deployer

The Application Deployer is responsible for managing the execution of user applications; similar to *brokers* in the Grid literature [2, 58, 108]. However, compared to brokers, the Application Deployer has more knowledge and control of the application tasks, being able to perform application-level scheduling, for example, for parameter sweeping executions [37]. It provides an application interface to the users and simplifies the processes of transferring application input data to each VM, starting the execution, and collecting the results from the VMs to the front-end node. The mapping of application tasks to VMs is performed by a scheduler located in the Application Deployer. After deploying application on the VMs, the application deployer stores the VM IDs, which is used by the monitoring component to identify the VMs to monitor.

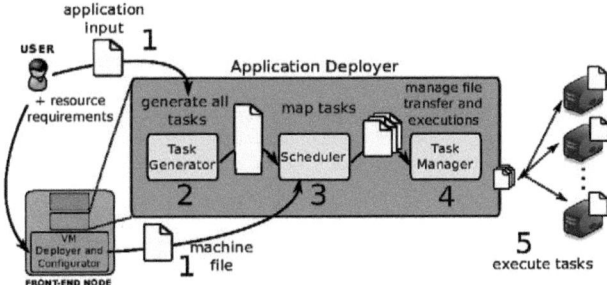

Figure 3.10: Application Deployer.

Figure 3.10 illustrates the main modules of the Application Deployer. The *task generator* integrated with the application interface receives from the user the application and its parameters, and at the same time the VM deployer generates a machine file based on user requirements (step 1). The *scheduler* uses this machine file and a list of all tasks (step 2) to map tasks to VMs (step 3). Each VM contains an executor, which requests tasks from the *task manager* whenever the executors are idle and there are tasks to be executed, thus allowing a dynamic load balancing (step 4). The *task manager* is also responsible for triggering the task executions on VMs (step 5) and collecting the results when tasks complete.

Automated Emulation Framework

The Automated Emulation Framework (AEF) was originally conceived for automated configuration and execution of emulation experiments [33]. Nevertheless, it can also be used to set up arbitrary virtual environments by not activating the emulated wide-area network support. In the latter case AEF works as a virtualized infrastructure manager, similar to tools such as OpenNebula [166], Oracle VM Manager [142], and OpenPEX [177].

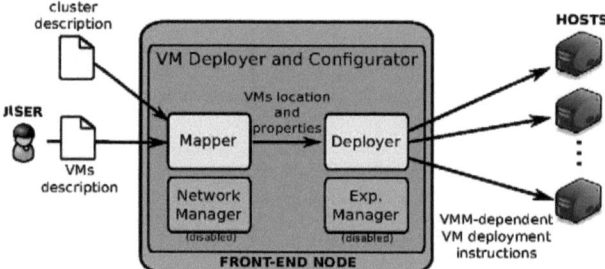

Figure 3.11: Automated Emulation Framework Overview.

Figure 3.11 depicts the architecture of the AEF framework. AEF input consists of two configuration files providing XML description of both the physical and virtual infrastructures. Using this information, AEF maps VMs to physical hosts. AEF supports different algorithms for VM mapping. The algorithm used in this work tries to reduce the number of hosts used by consolidating VMs as long as one host has enough resources to host several VMs. At the end of the mapping process, the resulting mapping is sent to the Deployer, which creates VMs in the hosts accordingly.

If network configuration is required in the environment (e.g., to create virtual networks), the Network Manager component of AEF performs this activity. Execution of the applications may be triggered either by the user, in case of interactive applications, or directly by AEF in case of non-interactive applications. In the experiments presented in Section 7.3, we opted for the former approach where the execution is triggered by the application deployer. VMs can be deployed via cluster front-end and then users can log in the machine and interact with the application.

3.7 DeSVi Implementation Strategies

In this section, we describe the implementation choices for each *DeSVi* component. To realize the components, we incorporated, whenever possible, well-established and tested open source tools in the implementations.

Application Deployer

The Application Deployer is written in Java and has as input a machine file (in plain ASCII format), which contains the list of hostnames or IPs of the VMs allocated to the user application and a task generator Java class to split the work to be done into a lists of tasks. For a rendering application, for instance, such a class includes a list of frames and the command to render them. The division of tasks per VM is performed by the Application Deployer's scheduler as described in Section 3.6.

The Application Deployer uses *scp*, a standard tool for copying files among multiple machines, in order to transfer the application-related files from the front-end node to VMs responsible for executing tasks. The *ssh* command is responsible for triggering an executor on each VM specified in the machine file. Each executor requests tasks to be executed from the task manager. During the user application execution, the Application Deployer generates log files with the time required to execute each task. After tasks executions are completed, the results are transferred back to the front-end node via *scp*. This model was chosen because it provides a reliable mechanism for file transferring (*scp*) together with persistent logging information that does not depend on a DBMS to archive results. The overall result of the approach is a reliable and lightweight mechanism for managing tasks that has an insignificant overhead on the platform, which is a requirement of a system aiming at managing QoS of resources.

Virtual Machine Deployer and Configurator

The automated emulation framework used to deploy and configure the virtual machines is implemented in Java. The framework inputs are XML files describing the characteristics of both, the required virtual machines and the cluster. Once these files are parsed, the Mapper component maps the virtual machines to the cluster nodes. During this stage, AEF ensures that the resources required by all virtual machines assigned to a cluster node do not exceed the node's available resources.

Once the mapping is finished, the resulting configuration is applied in the cluster by the VM Deployer component. Here, a parallel standalone deployer, which is part of the AEF core, is used. This parallel deployer module does not require external tools or systems for its operation, and it works as follows. First, a base image file of the virtual machines is copied, via *scp*, to each cluster node (as determined by the Mapper) simultaneously. This image contains all the software and configuration required by the application. After the base image is copied to each physical machine, it is replicated there to achieve the number of virtual images intended to be deployed on this specific physical machine. This step is also carried out simultaneously on each physical machine.

The replicated images are configured with VM-specific settings, such as hostname and static IP address. Finally, virtual machines are simultaneously created on each host from each image file replicated in the previous step. Furthermore, the deployer checks if an image is already present in a host before performing the transfer. Thus, if the image is already present in the host, the transfer process is skipped in such a host, saving bandwidth for the transfer of images in other hosts. Moreover, if the replicated VM images on each host are newer than the base image in use, the replication process is skipped. AEF is lightweight and supports deployment of systems based on Xen with negligible overhead. Moreover, its parallel transfer of VMs and selective replication of images reduces the amount of time required for building, and the deployment of virtual environments.

We present the evaluations of the DeSVi architecture in Section 7.3. We show in the evaluation the efficiency of the architecture in detecting SLA violations and in determining optimal measurement interval.

CHAPTER 4

SLA-Aware Application Scheduling

In the previous chapter, we addressed the issue of enforcing the SLA of application executing alone on a Cloud infrastructure. However, deploying one application per virtual machine is costly and might cause under-utilization of resources. Considering that one of the basic features attracting customers to the Cloud is low cost of application provisioning. Thus, the Cloud provider needs more appropriate scheduling and deployment strategies to achieve low cost, avoid resource wastage, and ensure the application performance.

In this chapter, we extend the Cloud management infrastructure with an SLA-aware application scheduling heuristic. We present a motivating scenario for the development of the scheduling heuristic after which, we present the detail design and implementation of the heuristic.

4.1 Scheduling Approach Motivation

Currently, many Cloud customer are interested in cost-effectively deploying single applications in Clouds. This is a situation common in the Software as a Service (SaaS) delivery model. Numerous commercial Cloud providers such as *salesforce.com* [157] are offering the provision of single applications based on agreed SLA terms. However, these commercial providers use custom techniques, which are not open to the general public. Therefore, to foster competitive Cloud market and reduce cost, there are need for open solutions. In the next section, we present a use case scenario showing the motivation for our open source scheduling solution.

Use Case Scenario

Figure 4.1 presents a motivating scenario for the development of our scheduling and deployment heuristic.

The use case scenario shows a Cloud provider and a pools of customers who wish to deploy their applications on the Cloud resources based on the pre-agreed SLA objectives. The challenge now is how to deploy these application on the available virtual machines in the Cloud to ensure

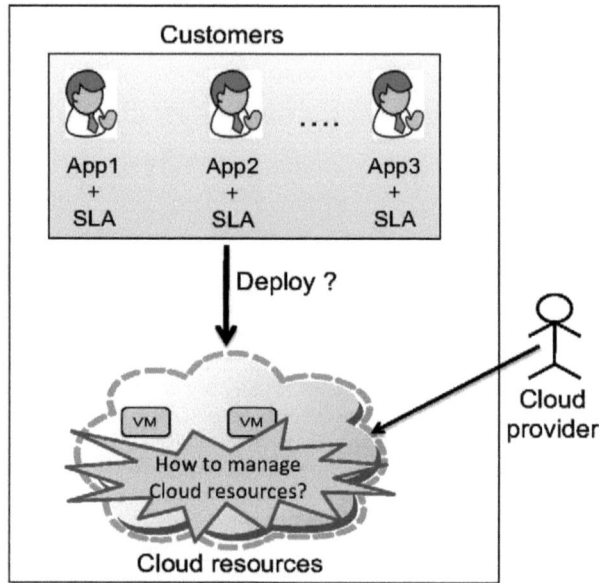

Figure 4.1: Scheduling Motivation Scenario

their performance and enforce the agreed SLA objectives. Furthermore, another challenge is how to manage resources to achieve high utilizations and maximum deployments.

To address these challenges, we present a novel scheduling heuristic considering multiple SLA parameter objectives, such as amount of required CPU, network bandwidth, and storage in deploying applications on Clouds. The heuristic includes a load-balancing mechanism for efficient distribution of the applications' execution on the Cloud resources. We also present a flexible on-demand resource allocation strategy included in the heuristic for automatically starting new virtual machines (VM) when a non-appropriate VM is available for application deployment. We discuss the concept and detailed design of the heuristic including its implementation in the CloudSim simulation tool [32, 34].

The scheduling strategy proposed in this section is integrated into the LoM2HiS framework as shown in Figure 4.2.

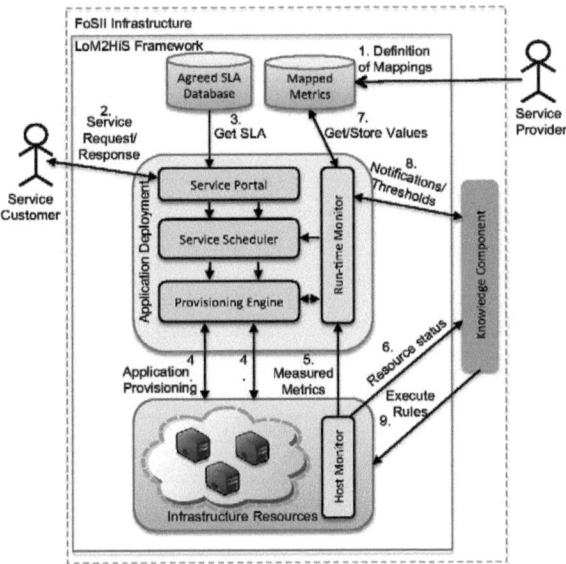

Figure 4.2: LoM2HiS with Scheduling Strategy

4.2 Resource Provisioning and Application Deployment Models

The idea of Cloud computing is to provide resources as a service in a flexible and scalable manner [31]. There are three well known types of resource provisioning [90, 147] in Clouds: i) *Infrastructure as a Service (IaaS)* that offers bare hardwares such as the physical machines, storage devices, and network infrastructures as a service. Amazon EC2 [6] is an example of *IaaS* offering; ii) *Platform as a Service (PaaS)*, which delivers platform for application development and deployment as a service. It typically utilizes virtualized resources in form of virtual machines that are capable of provisioning resources to applications. A typical example of *PaaS* service is the Google App Engine [85]; and iii) *Software as a Service (SaaS)* offering resources for the provisioning of single applications in a Cloud environment. Vendors of *SaaS* include *salesforce.com* [157].

The Cloud provisioning and deployment model presented in Figure 4.3 shows a scenario combining the three different types of resource provisioning to host service requested from customers. The customers place their service deployment requests to the service portal (step 1 in Figure 4.3), which passes the requests to the request processing component to validate the requests (step 2). If the request is validated, it is then forwarded to the scheduler (step 3). The scheduler selects the appropriate VMs through the provisioning engine in *PaaS* layer for de-

35

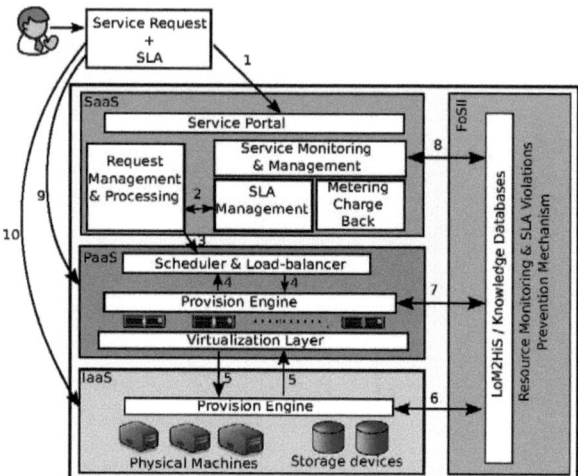

Figure 4.3: Cloud Provisioning and Deployment Model.

ploying the requested service and the load-balancer balances the service provisioning among the running VMs (step 4). The provision engine manages the VMs on the virtualization layer and the virtualization layer interacts with the physical resources via the provision engine in *IaaS* layer (step 5).

The low-level resource metrics of the physical resources at the *IaaS* layer are monitored by the *LoM2HiS* framework [60] (step 6). We use the knowledge management component [131] to provide reactive actions in case of SLA violations (step 7). The service status and the SLA information are communicated back to the service portal (step 8).

Although, the scenario described above is a possible way of combining the three types of resource provisioning, there exist other scenarios like provisioning of virtual machines alone (step 9) and provisioning of physical resources alone (step 10), which are possibilities of provisioning at the single layers alone.

However, our approach aims to provide an integrated resource provisioning strategy. Thus, our proposed scheduling heuristics considers the three layers. Efficient resource provisioning and application deployments at these layers are not trivial considering their different constraints and requirements. At the *IaaS* layer the physical resources must be managed to optimize utilizations. At the *PaaS* layer, the VMs have to be deployed and maintained on the physical host considering the agreed SLAs with the customer. Deploying single applications at *SaaS* layer is challenging due to the fact that each application demands the fulfillment of its SLA terms. In the next section we discuss our proposed scheduling heuristic aimed to address these challenges.

4.3 Scheduling and Load Balancing Mechanisms

The proposed scheduling heuristic [59] aims at deploying applications on virtual machines based on the agreed SLA objectives. With this strategy, the possibility of violating the SLA objectives are highly reduced thereby optimizing the performance of the applications, and increasing the profits of the Cloud provider, since he does not need to pay costly SLA violation penalties. Moreover, the integrated load-balancer in the heuristic ensures high and efficient resource utilization, consequently saving the provider the cost of maintaining unused resources.

In this work, we assume that the SLA terms between the customer and the Cloud provider are already established. Thus, the processes of SLA specification, negotiation, and establishment are out of scope for this work, but there are ongoing research work where the *VieSLAF framework* [24] is used to address the issues.

1: Input: UserServiceRequest
2: get *globalResourcesAndAvailableVmList*;
3: // find appropriateVMList
4: **if** $AP(R, AR) != \emptyset$ **then**
5:     //call the load balancing algorithm
6:     *deployableVm* = load-balance($AP(R, AR)$);
7:     deploy *service* on *deployableVm*;
8:     *deployed* = true;
9: **else**
10:     **if** *globalResourceAbleToHostExtraVM* **then**
11:         start *newVMInstance*;
12:         add *VMToAvailableVMList*;
13:         deploy *service* on *newVm*;
14:         *deployed* = true;
15:     **else**
16:         queue *serviceRequest* until
17:         *queueTime* > *waitingTime*
18:         *deployed* = false;
19:     **end if**
20: **end if**
21: **if** *deployed* **then**
22:     return *successful*;
23:     terminate;
24: **else**
25:     return *failure*;
26:     terminate;
27: **end if**

Algorithm 4.1: Scheduling Heuristic

According to the pseudocode presented in Algorithm 4.1, the scheduler receives as input the customers' service requests (R) that are composed of the SLA objectives (S) and the application data (A) to be provisioned (line 1 in Algorithm 4.1). The request can be expressed as $R = (S, A)$. Each SLA agreement has a unique identifier id and a collection of SLA Objectives (SLOs). The SLOs can be defined as predicates of the form:

$$SLO_{id}(x_i, comp, \pi_i) \text{ with } comp \in \{<, \leq, >, \geq, =\} \tag{4.1}$$

where $x_i \in \{Bandwidth, Memory, Storage, Availability\}$ represents sample SLA parameters, $comp$ the appropriate comparison operator, and π_i the values of the objectives.

The output of the scheduler is the confirmation of successful deployment or error message in case of failure. In the first step, it extracts the SLA objectives, which forms the basis for finding the virtual machine with the appropriate resources for deploying the application. Next, it gathers information about the total available resources (AR) and the number of running virtual machines in the data center (line 2). The SLA objectives are used to find a list of appropriate virtual machines (AP) capable of provisioning the requested service (R). This operation can be expressed as

$$AP(R, AR) = \{VM : VM \in AR, capable(VM, R)\} \tag{4.2}$$

where $capable(VM, R)$ is a predicate that returns true if the virtual machine is capable of provisioning the particular request or false otherwise (lines 3-4). Once the list of VMs are found, the load-balancer decides on which particular VM to deploy the application in order to balance the load in the data center (lines 5-8).

In case there is no VM with the appropriate resources running in the data center, the scheduler checks if the global resources consisting of physical machines can host new VMs (lines 9-10). If that is the case, it automatically starts new VMs with predefined resource capacities to provision service requests (lines 11-14). When the global resources cannot host extra VMs, the scheduler queues the provisioning of service requests until a VM with appropriate resources is available (lines 15-16). If after a certain period of time, the service requests cannot be scheduled and deployed, the scheduler returns a scheduling failure to the Cloud admin, otherwise it returns success (lines 17-27).

The load-balancer is presented in Algorithm 4.2. Its working strategy is similar to that of the Next-Fit algorithm [92], which in an array of boxes fills each box one after the other and never goes back to the filled boxes. The load-balancer as shown in Algorithm 4.2 is not an extension of Next-Fit algorithm and has two core differences to it: i) it does not fill a box to the full before starting to fill another one and ii) it goes back to the half filled boxes to add new items. Their similarity lies in the fact that in each iteration, it does not put items in the last filled box unless there is no other appropriate box among all the boxes.

As shown in Algorithm 4.2, the load balancer receives as input the appropriate VM list (line 1 in Algorithm 4.2). In its operations, it first gets the number of available running VMs in the data center in order to know how to balance the load among them (line 2). In the next step, it gets a list of used VMs, i.e., VMs that are already provisioning applications (line 3). If this list is equal to the number of running VMs, it clears the list because that means all the VMs are currently provisioning some applications (lines 4-7). Therefore, the first VM from the appropriate VM list can be selected for the deployment of the new application request. The selected VM is then added to the list of used VMs so that the load-balancer does not select it in the next iteration (lines 8-15).

1: Input: $AP(R, AR)$
2: globalvariable *availableVmList*
3: globalvariable *usedVmList*;
4: *deployableVm* = null;
5: **if** *size(usedVMList) == size(availableVmList)* **then**
6:    clear *usedVmList*;
7: **end if**
8: **for** *vm* in $AP(R, AR)$ **do**
9:    **if** *vm* not in *usedVmList* **then**
10:      add *vm* to *usedVmList*;
11:      *deployableVm* = *vm*;
12:      break;
13:    **end if**
14: **end for**
15: return *deployableVm*;

Algorithm 4.2: Load Balancing Strategy

The load-balancer tries to place one application on each VM running in the data center in the first phase after which it goes back again to place new applications on the VMs. The idea is that VMs executing less number of applications perform better than ones executing many applications while the others are running empty.

The load-balancer alone has a total worst-case complexity of $0(n^2)$ in load-balancing and selecting the specific VM for application deployment. This worst-case complexity is attributed by two processes: i) by the processes of selecting the specific VM, which has a worst-case complexity of $0(n)$ because the load balancer in worst case has to go through the appropriate VM list of n size to select a specific VM; and ii) by the processes of balancing the load among the VMs, which has a worse-case complexity of $0(n)$. As shown in Algorithm 4.2 lines 8-14, this process is a sub-process of selecting the specific VM. Thus, the total worst-case complexity is of $0(n^2)$.

The scheduling heuristic without the load-balancer has a worst-case complexity of $0(m+n)$. This complexity is defined by the processes of finding out the resource capacities of the m physical machines and n available virtual machines in the data center. Other operations of the heuristic have constant complexity $(0(1))$ except the process of checking for available resources on the physical machines in order to start new VMs, which has a worst-case complexity of $0(m)$.

Therefore, the total worst-case complexity of the proposed heuristic is a result of the sum of the scheduling heuristic complexity and the load-balancer complexity, which can be expressed as follows

$$0(m+n) + 0(n^2) = 0(n^2 + m). \tag{4.3}$$

As shown by Equation 4.3, the proposed scheduling heuristic is polynomial at runtime.

4.4 Implementation Issues

The proposed scheduling heuristic is implemented as a new scheduling policy in the CloudSim simulation tool for the purpose of evaluation. CloudSim is a scalable simulation tool offering features like: i) support for modeling and simulation of large scale Cloud computing environments including data centers, on a single computing machine; ii) a self-contained platform for modeling Clouds, service brokers, resource provisioning and application allocation policies; iii) capability of simulating network connections among simulated components; and iv) support for simulation of federated Cloud environment able to network resources from both private and public providers. Furthermore, CloudSim possesses two unique features: i) availability of virtualization engine that aids in creation and management of multiple, independent, and co-hosted virtualized services on a data center's physical machine; and ii) ability to switch between space-shared and time-shared allocation of CPU cores to virtualized resources. The above mentioned features of CloudSim help accelerate development of new application provisioning algorithms for Cloud computing. Further information about CloudSim can be found in [34].

In the next section, we describe the scheduling heuristic implementation together with the custom extensions made to the CloudSim tool.

Custom Extensions and Scheduler Implementation

We extended CloudSim with the components shown in the *custom extensions layer* as presented in Figure 4.4. The infrastructure level services are modeled by the *core layer* representing the original CloudSim data center, which encapsulates sets of computing hosts that can either be homogeneous or heterogeneous with respect to the configuration of their hardware (CPU cores, bandwidth, storage, memory). Each data center instantiates a resource provisioning component that implements a set of policies that allocates resources to computing host and virtual machines.

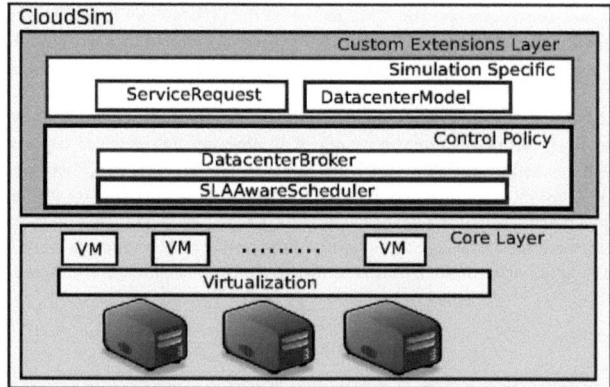

Figure 4.4: CloudSim Extension Architecture.

Our extensions to CloudSim is divided into two groups of Java classes: i) the *control policy* classes; and ii) the *simulation specific* classes. The *control policy* classes include the implementations of a new *data center broker* for interfacing with the data center and our proposed scheduling heuristic. The *data center broker* is responsible for mediating negotiations between customers and Cloud providers in respect of allocating appropriate resources to customer services to meet their application's QoS needs and to manage the provider resources in the CloudSim. Our extended *data center broker* includes the capability of running dynamic simulations thereby removing the burden of statically configuring the whole simulation scenario before starting the simulation. With this feature one can generate and send in new events (service requests) during the simulation runtime.

The proposed scheduling heuristic provides policies used by the *data center broker* for allocating resources to applications. The implementations of the heuristic and that of the load-balancer are realized with Java methods in a class named *SLAAwareScheduler* as shown in Figure 4.4. This class is used by the *DatacenterBroker* class to schedule, deploy applications, and manage the data center resources.

The *simulation specific* classes are used in realizing simulation scenarios. This group includes two Java classes named *DatacenterModel* and *ServiceRequest* as shown in Figure 4.4. The *DatacenterModel* class presents methods for flexible instantiation of different data center scenarios for scalable simulations. We used this class in our evaluations to easily configure and evaluate different scenarios. The *ServiceRequest* class represents a customer service request. It encapsulates information about the SLA parameter objectives agreed between the customer and the provider and the application data to be provisioned in the Cloud.

We present in Section 7.4 the evaluation of the scheduling heuristic. The evaluation demonstrate the achievable resource utilization efficiency and we explained the obtained results.

CHAPTER 5

Cloud Application Monitoring

In the previous chapter, we discussed the scheduling heuristic to schedule and deploy multiple applications on single virtual machines based on their service level agreement objectives. The application behaviour at runtime might change at any point in time making it difficult to ensure the agreed SLA objectives. To address this issue the provider needs advanced monitoring capabilities.

In this chapter, we extend the Cloud management infrastructure with application monitoring techniques. We first describe the motivation scenario for the development of the monitoring architecture. In the next step, we discuss the design concepts and the implementation of the architecture.

5.1 Application Monitoring Motivation

To establish Cloud computing as a reliable state of the art form of on-demand computing, Cloud providers have to offer scalability, reliable resources, competitive prices, and minimize interactions with the customers in case of failures or environmental changes. However, ensuring SLA for different Cloud customers at the application layer is not a trivial task. Monitoring at this layer is necessary as several applications may share the same VMs (*e.g.,* to reduce energy consumption and cost) or one application may run on multiple VMs (*e.g.,* large scale distributed or parallel applications). In the next section, we present a motivating use case scenario for the development of this monitoring architecture.

Use Case Scenario

The use case scenario describes a Cloud environment where multiple customer applications are being consolidated and provisioned on the same virtual machine. Figure 5.1 present a graphical overview of the scenario.

In the use case scenario, each application is being provisioned based on the individual agreed SLA objectives. Thus, how can the provider guarantee these SLA objectives respec-

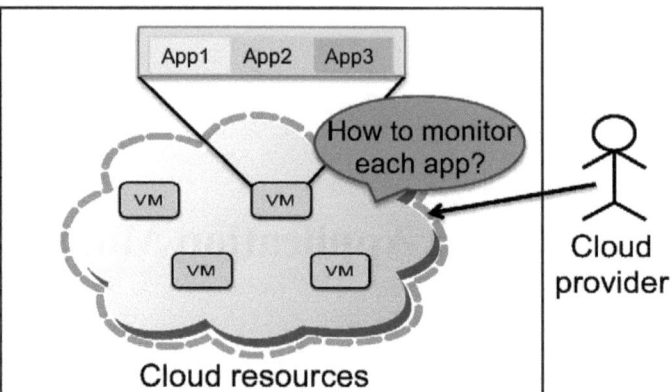

Figure 5.1: CASViD Motivating Scenario.

tively to avoid violations and the payments of penalties via monitoring? Furthermore, how can the provider automatically determine the optimal measurement intervals for efficient monitoring of the applications?

To solve this problem, we propose CASViD (Cloud Application SLA Violations Detection) architecture for efficient monitoring and SLA violation detection at the application provisioning layer in Clouds. Its core component is the application-level monitor, which is capable of monitoring application metrics at runtime to determine their resource consumption behaviours and performance. The research contributions of this architecture are: (i) the conceptual design of the application monitoring techniques, (ii) the build-up, design, and integration of the CASViD components, (iii) description of the implementation choices for the architecture, and (iv) the presentation of an algorithm for investigating the optimal measurement interval for monitoring different application types.

5.2 CASViD Design Concept

CASViD (Cloud Application SLA Violations Detection) architecture is capable of monitoring single customer application to determine its performance status and thereby check for SLA violation situations (Figure 5.2).

Customers place their service requests through a defined interface to the front-end node (step 1, Figure 5.2), which acts as the management node in the Cloud environment. The VM configurator sets up the Cloud environment by deploying preconfigured VM images (step 2) on physical machines and making them accessible for service provisioning. The customer request is

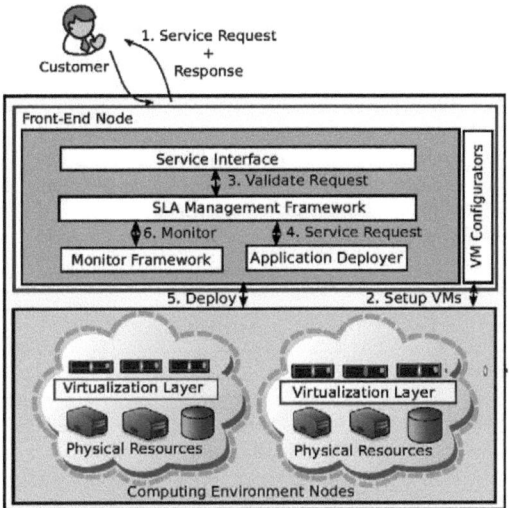

Figure 5.2: CASViD Architecture Overview.

received by the service interface and delivered to the SLA management framework for validation (step 3), which is done to ensure that the request comes from the right customer. In the next step the service request is passed to the application deployer (step 4), which allocates resources for the service execution and deploys it in the Cloud environment (step 5). After deploying the service application, CASViD monitors the application execution and sends the monitored information to the SLA management framework (step 6) for processing and detection of SLA violations.

The VM configurator and application deployer are components for allocating resources and deploying applications on our Cloud testbed. They are included in the architecture to show our complete solution.

The proposed CASViD architecture is generic in its usage as it is not designed for a particular set of applications. The service interface supports the provisioning of transactional as well as computational applications. The SLA management framework can handle the provisioning of all application types based on the pre-negotiated SLAs. Description of the negotiation process and components is out of scope of this thesis and is discussed by Brandic *et al.* [23].

System and Application Monitor

CASViD architecture contains a flexible monitoring framework based on the SNMP (Simple Network Management Protocol) standard [38]. It receives instructions to monitor applications

45

from the SLA management framework and delivers the monitored information. Its design is based on the traditional manager/agent model used in network management. Figure 5.3 presents the monitor architecture. The manager, located in the management node, polls periodically each agent in the cluster to get the monitored information. In order to enhance its scalability, the monitor uses asynchronous communication with all cluster agents. It is composed of a library and an agent. The monitor agent implements the methods to capture each metric defined in the CASViD monitor MIB (Management Information Base). At the manager side, the monitor library provides methods to configure which metrics should be captured and which nodes should be included in the monitoring. The SLA management framework in the system architecture uses this library to configure the monitoring process and retrieve the desired metrics.

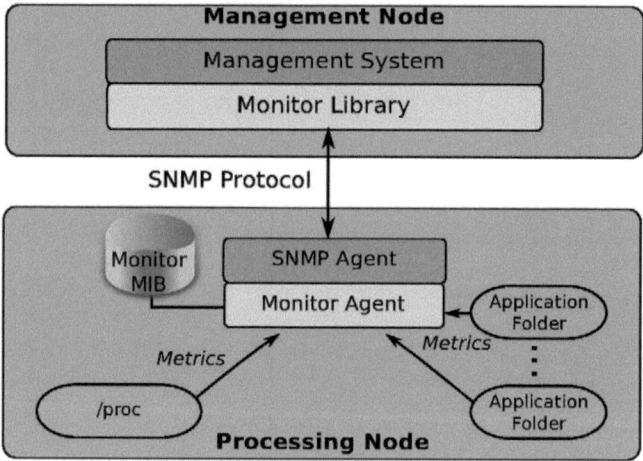

Figure 5.3: CASViD Monitor Overview.

Similar to other monitoring systems [72, 129], CASViD monitor is general purpose and supports the acquisition of common application metrics, and even system metrics such as CPU and memory utilization. The application metrics (SLA parameters) to be monitored depends on the application type and how to ensure its performance.

SLA Management Framework

The service provisioning management and detection of application SLA objective violations are performed by the SLA management framework component. This component is central and interacts with the Service Interface, Application Deployer, and CASViD monitor. In order to manage the SLA violations, it receives the monitored information from the monitoring agents embedded in the computing nodes where the applications are executing. The management framework is designed to access the SLA database containing the originally agreed SLAs between the customer and the provider. It retrieves from this database the SLA objectives, which are used together with predefined thresholds to detect SLA violation situations.

The strategy of detecting SLA violations is based on the use of predefined violation thresholds. A violation threshold is a value indicating the least acceptable performance level for an application. For example *Response time* $\leq 2ms$. In this case, $2ms$ is the violation threshold.

Exceeding the violation threshold values indicates the occurrence of SLA violations. With this information the system can react quickly to avert the violation threat and save the provider from costly SLA violation penalties. In case the violation threat cannot be averted and the real violation situation persists, the system logs the necessary information for calculating the appropriate SLA violation penalties.

Algorithm for Obtaining Optimal Intervals

The proposed CASViD architecture can be used in several Cloud management scenarios. For example to facilitate the execution of multiple applications on a single computing node to reduce cost and save energy in a Cloud environment. CASViD can also assist management systems to migrate applications between computing nodes in order to shutdown some nodes to save energy. The applications normally belong to different customers and are provisioned based on their agreed SLA objectives. The architecture measures the resource consumption and performance of each application to detect SLA violations. In order to achieve this, there is a need of finding an interval for optimal measurements.

The optimal measurement interval depends on the application and its input and such interval has to be determined automatically. Thus, the provider can automatically select the optimal measurement interval for each independent application by sampling different intervals until the provider utility gets stable. Algorithm 5.1 presents the pseudo-code for obtaining the optimal measurement interval.

```
1  intervalList ← set list of possible intervals
2  optimalInterval ← intervalList[0]
3  maxTime ← MAXTIME
4  netUtility ← 0
5  for ∀interval ∈ intervalList do
6      tmpNetUtility ← monitorApp(maxTime)
7      if tmpNetUtility > netUtility then
8          netUtility ← tmpNetUtility
9          optimalInterval ← interval
10     end
11 end
12 return optimalInterval
```
Algorithm 5.1: Pseudo-code for Obtaining Optimal Measurement Intervals.

As presented in Algorithm 5.1, the variables are first initialized (lines 1-4). Then the algorithm evaluates each interval to find the optimal one (line 5). The algorithm uses each interval to monitor the application for a maximum specified time (line 6) after which it checks if the net utility gained with the current interval is higher than the highest net utility so far (line 7). If yes, this net utility gain becomes the highest net utility (line 8) and this interval is set to be the current optimal interval (line 9). If no, the previous highest net utility is retained. The algorithm goes back to step 5 and checks the other interval using the same procedure. At the end, the interval with the highest net utility is returned as the optimal measurement interval (line 10). The calculation of the net utility is described in Section 7.5.

5.3 Implementation Choices

This section presents the implementation choices and decision for the CASViD architecture. The implementation aims at fulfilling some of the Cloud computing requirements such as scalability, efficiency, and reliability.

CASViD Monitor

The CASViD monitor uses the SNMP protocol for the communication between the manager and the agent in each cluster node. It is composed of a library and an agent. The monitor library is implemented in Java and uses the SNMP4J library[1], which provides access to all functionalities of the SNMP protocol for Java applications. The monitor uses version 2c of the SNMP protocol to communicate with the agents. The communication is performed using asynchronous requests to enhance the scalability. Each request to an agent creates a listener process, which is automatically called when the message arrives.

The CASViD monitor agent is implemented in Python and receives the SNMP request through the net-snmp daemon[2] that is installed in each node. The net-snmp daemon forwards all requests for the metrics defined in the CASViD monitor MIB to the monitor agent. The monitor agent periodically processes the requests, which are instructions to probe the application metrics. These metrics are obtained through the standard /proc directory, which enables the gathering of kernel information regarding the underlying system including current configuration and performance metrics. The capture of application metrics is performed by identifying the process ID executing the application and its log files. The monitoring agent accesses the files to get the application specific metrics and the obtained results are packaged in an SNMP message and sent back to the manager by the net-snmp daemon.

We used SNMP in the CASViD monitor to realize a generic solution deployable in various platforms and operating systems. SNMP is well established, and even many hardware devices today are being managed based on SNMP protocol.

CASViD SLA Management Framework

The whole framework is implemented in Java language. To realize the SLA violation detection, it interacts with the monitor through a defined interface where it receives a data structure holding

---

[1] SNMP4j - Free Open Source SNMP API for Java - http://www.snmp4j.org/
[2] Net-SNMP - http://www.net-snmp.org

the metric-value pairs monitored by the monitor agents. With the metric-value pairs, it builds a message buffer for the Java Messaging Service (JMS) [97]. The JMS is used together with Apache ActiveMQ [3] to realize a scalable communication mechanism for the framework.

The message passes through ESPER engine [69], which filters out identical monitored values so that only changed values between measurements are delivered for the evaluations against the predefined violation thresholds. The filtering reduces the number of messages to be processed in order to increase the scalability of the framework. We use MySQL DB to store the processed messages. In this respect, we use HIBERNATE to map our Java classes into DB tables for easy storing and retrieving of information.

This framework is implemented to be highly scalable. JMS and ActiveMQ are used because they are platform independent and due to the scalability of the underlying ActiveMQ queues. Furthermore, the application of ESPER to filter out identical monitored information reduces drastically the number of messages to be processed. Especially in situations where the agents are monitoring in short intervals.

The evaluation of the CASViD architecture is presented in Section 7.5. It shows the ability of the architecture to monitor and detect application SLA violations. Furthermore, it demonstrate the strategy of automatically determining the optimal measurement interval for application monitoring.

CHAPTER 6

Holistic Monitoring and Management of Provisioning Lifecycle

In this chapter, we discuss the usage of the proposed Cloud management infrastructure with the help of a case study. We first discuss the holistic monitoring concept. In the next step, we introduce the knowledge management techniques, which provide the autonomic behaviour capabilities to our management infrastructure. And finally, we present the details of the case study, which include an overview of scientific workflows and RNA sequencing in bioinformatics.

6.1 Holistic Monitoring Concept

The term 'holistic' expresses the importance of a whole solution rather than part solutions. This concept is being applied in different areas such as in business process engineering [128, 173], e-government [125, 183, 184], health [16, 100], and engineering [4, 82].

In this thesis, we apply this concept to the monitoring techniques to express the coverage and ability of our contributed monitoring solutions. Because, in this work, we designed and implemented two monitoring techniques to monitor at infrastructure- and application-layers in Clouds. As we have discussed earlier, monitoring alone, at the infrastructure layer or at the application layer, is not sufficient for the efficient management of Cloud environments. Thus, the combination of the two monitoring techniques to achieve a holistic monitoring solution for the proposed Cloud management infrastructure.

6.2 Knowledge Management techniques

In this section, we present knowledge management techniques that utilizes the monitored information to provide proactive actions for resource and application management operations. The knowledge management techniques are used for the autonomic execution of operations such as resource allocation, resource deallocation, and virtual machine migration. It provides autonomic behaviours for the proposed Cloud management infrastructure.

The term knowledge management (KM) in our context, means intelligent usage of measured data, obtained by monitoring, for the decision making process to satisfy application performance goal defined in SLA agreements while optimizing the computational resource usage. Apart from the monitoring phase (as shown in Figure 6.1), the knowledge management consist of three other phases namely *analysis*, *plan*, and *execute*. The core of the KM is a knowledge database that interacts with these phases in the management process.

Figure 6.1 presents an overview of our knowledge management approach. The monitoring phase delivers the monitored information, which include details about the actual resource allocation status, the utilization of the resources by the workflow applications, and the applications' performance goal defined in the SLA. The *analysis* phase processes the monitored data. It provides an interface for receiving the monitored information from the monitoring phase. It analyzes the received information to determine the exact application SLA violation threshold that is violated, and then decides on the exact reactive action to carry out in order to prevent a future SLA violation. The *plan* phase plans the execution of the recommended actions and prevents oscillation effects (i.e., allocating and deallocating the same resource interchangeably) in the operations. This phase is divided into two parts: *plan I* and *plan II*. Plan I is responsible for mapping actions onto physical and virtual machines in the Cloud environments and managing those machines. *Plan II* is in charge of planning the order and timing of the actions. The *execute* phase is the final one. It executes the recommended actions on the computational devices with the help of software actuators.

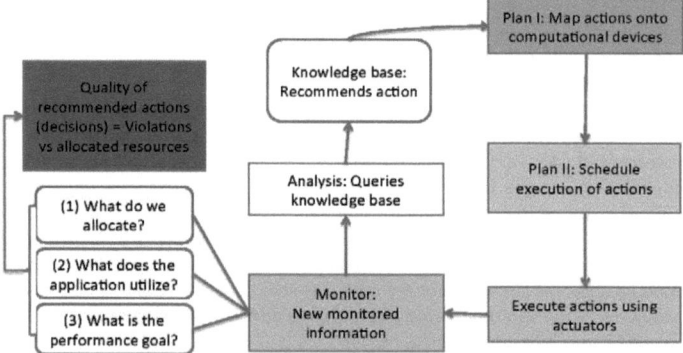

Figure 6.1: Knowledge Management Overview

We have successfully applied different techniques such as Case-Based Reasoning (briefly described in Section 2.1), rule-based, etc for knowledge management in Cloud environments [131–133]. In the next section, we show how we integrated monitoring with knowledge management techniques in a case study to optimize workflow application execution.

6.3 Case Study: Integrating Monitoring with Knowledge Management

This section presents a case study where we apply the proposed Cloud management infrastructure, which consist of monitoring- and knowledge management aspects to facilitate the execution of bioinformatic workflow application. The objectives of this case study are: i) the application of Cloud management techniques to workflow applications; ii) the management of scientific workflow application execution to support their successful completions using Cloud features; and iii) the evaluation of our approach, which is demonstrated using TopHat [175], a typical scientific workflow application from the field of bioinformatics that exemplifies the challenges in the complex analysis of large data sets from modern high-throughput technologies.

In this case study, we first present an overview of scientific workflow and its challenges. In a further step, we give some background information on bioinformatic research area, RNA sequencing, and the TopHat workflow application after which, we present the monitoring of workflow execution and the application of resource management techniques. This case study is based on our work presented in [64].

Scientific Workflow Overview and Challenges

A workflow can be defined as a composite task that comprises coordinated human and machine executed sub-tasks [109]. In computer aided scientific work, a scientific workflow application is a holistic unit that defines, executes, and manages sub-task processes with the help of software artifacts [93].

Scientific workflow applications have become an empowering tool for large-scale data analysis in bioinformatics [154, 165], providing the necessary abstractions that enable effective usage of computational and data resources. They also strive to manage their operation complexities to free researchers to focus on guiding the data analysis, interpretation of results, and taking decisions whenever human inputs are required [109].

Considering the fast development of high-throughput technologies, which generate huge amounts of data, scientific workflow applications can be instrumental in achieving automation and breaking down extended complexity in the life sciences [174]. The execution of workflow applications can be computationally intensive and requires reliable resource availability. Moreover, scientific workflow applications should be highly flexible to accommodate changes of input data and dynamical parameter modifications, even during execution.

The efficient management of such flexible workflow applications seeking to guarantee the availability of resources and the achievement of their performance goals is a challenging task. Often, resource availability decides the successful execution of a complex and expensive workflow application. Thus, there is a need for advanced techniques to monitor at runtime, the resource consumption behaviours and to inform about resource shortages, so that the management system can take adequate resource allocation decisions to support the successful completion of each workflow application.

Traditionally, a workflow application can be executed using local and distributed compute resources. Such resources are basically limited and, traditionally, cannot be dynamically reallocated. Considering that workflow applications are resource intensive and can take hours if not days to complete, provisioning them in an environment with fixed resources leads to poor performance and possible execution failures due to the lack of a flexible allocation of extra resources. The Cloud is proving to be a valuable complement to the compute resources, traditionally used in bioinformatics research laboratories [139]. Cloud computing technology promises on-demand and flexible resource provisioning that can be realized autonomically [31, 99]. The execution of workflow applications in a Cloud environment allows for easier management and guaranteeing of their performance goals.

Bioinformatics Background

Bioinformatics is the research discipline in which scientists, with the use of computational methods, seek to gain insights from data gathered in the life sciences [109]. An example is the discovery of interesting patterns in data obtained from laboratory experiments and/or from earlier results stored in databases that can be online, located in storage sites spread around the world. Bioinformatics is both applying established computational tools to new data, as well as new tools to well characterized data sets, seeking to improve on earlier methods. Thus, in bioinformatics, like in many modern research disciplines, scientific workflow applications empower advanced and more complex analysis. Previously, some management systems have been developed to facilitate the execution of workflow applications that use data and services from distributed sources [5, 55, 83, 96].

As a result of the proliferation of new high-throughput technologies in the life sciences that generate massive amounts of data, the retrieval, storage, and analysis of data face great technical challenges [152, 169]. In particular, often, bioinformatics tools, many of which are available only through web-based interfaces, are not suited for the analysis of newly generated large-scale data sets due to their computational intensiveness [35, 145]. In general, existing workflow application management systems cannot handle the massive amounts of data and execute workflow applications on these efficiently either [120]. New analysis software, workflow applications, monitoring, and management approaches are required that can take advantage of more powerful infrastructure such as compute clusters or Cloud environments.

Considering the Next Generation Sequencing (NGS), a recently introduced high-throughput technology for the identification of nucleotide molecules like RNA or DNA in biomedical samples. The output of the sequencing process is a list of billions of character sequences called 'reads', each typically holds up to 35-200 letters that represent the individual DNA bases determined. Lately, this technology has also been used to identify and count the abundances of RNA molecules that reflect new gene activity. We use the approach, called RNA-Seq, as a typical example of a scientific workflow application in the field of bioinformatics.

At first, in the analysis of RNA-Seq data, the obtained sequences are aligned to the reference genome. We apply the TopHat [175] aligner, consists of many sub-tasks, some of them executing sequentially, whereas the others run in parallel (Figure 6.2). These sub-tasks can have different resource-demand characteristics: needing extensive computational power, demanding high I/O access, or requiring extensive memory size.

In Figure 6.2, the nodes marked with * represent simplified sub-tasks of the workflow application, whereas the nodes marked with # represent the data transfered between the sub-tasks.

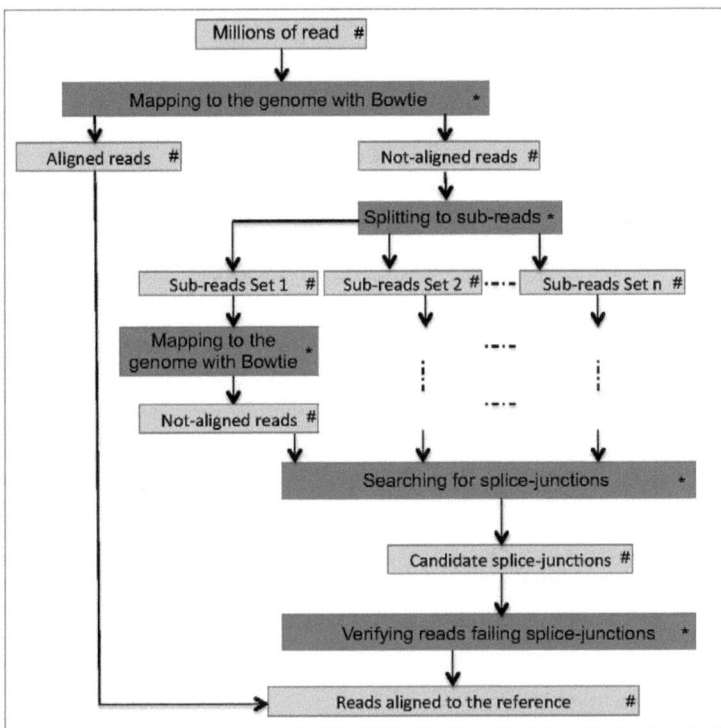

Figure 6.2: Overview of the TopHat Aligning Approach

The first sub-task aligns input reads to the given genome using the Bowtie program [112]. Unaligned reads are then divided into shorter sub-sequences that are further aligned to the reference genome in the next sub-task. If sub-sequences coming from the same read were aligned successfully to the genome, it may indicate that this read was straddling a 'gap' in the gene, falling on a so-called splice-junction. After verification of candidate reads falling on splice junctions, these and the reads that were aligned in the first sub-task are combined to create an output with a comprehensive list of localized alignments.

Workflow Application SLA Objectives

The provisioning of workflow application in a Cloud environment is to achieve certain performance goals as required by the bioinformatic scientist. As discussed in Section 6.3, bioinformatic workflow applications are resource intensive and take considerable time to complete their execution.

In this case study, we specify the performance goals for the bioinformatic workflow as SLA objectives, which are used by the management infrastructure to manage the execution of the TopHat workflow application used to analyze the RNA-Seq data. Table 6.1 depicts the service level agreement showing the performance objectives for the workflow application.

Table 6.1: Workflow SLA Objectives.

SLA Parameter	SLA Objective
CPU	90 %
Storage	19 GB
Memory	9 GB
Execution Status	Successful Completion

Table 6.1 shows the SLA objective requirements for the execution of the workflow application. The *CPU, memory,* and *storage* are the computational resource necessary for the execution and analysis of the RNA sequence data. The *execution status* objective for the workflow application is very essential. As discussed earlier, the execution time of the workflow application depends on the size of the RNA sequence data and the amount of computational resource available. Restarting the execution of failed RNA sequence data analysis due to lack of computational resources is highly time consuming and costly to bioinformatic scientist, therefore, it is very important to them to guarantee the continuous execution of the workflow application to reach successful completion.

Workflow Execution Monitoring

In this section, we present the holistic monitoring technique to monitor the execution of the workflow application and to report the resource and performance status. Scientific workflow applications are resource intensive and can take considerable amount of time to complete. The successful completion of data analysis using workflow applications in the life sciences is paramount to the scientist. To facilitate this objective, we apply our developed holistic monitoring techniques to monitor the workflow application executions in order to supervise the computational resource status.

Normally, workflow applications are composed of other applications (sub-tasks) linked together to achieve a common goal (as shown in Figure 6.2). A workflow application can be executed in a distributed system using multiple computational nodes in which case some parts of the application might execute on a different node. Thus, the successful completion of a workflow application depends on the completion of its composed parts.

To demonstrate our approach, we apply the Cloud management infrastrucuture to support scientific data analysis processes as shown in Figure 6.2. For simplicity and ease of understanding, we use a reduced version of Figure 6.2 in this demonstration.

As described in the early chapters, our monitoring techniques consist of components such as: i) the *Monitoring agents* that monitors single computational nodes; ii) the *Host monitor* that gathers and processes monitored information from the Monitoring agents; and iii) the *Run-time monitor* that maps metrics and monitors application SLAs. Figure 6.3 presents how we applied the monitoring components to efficiently manage the scientific data analysis processes.

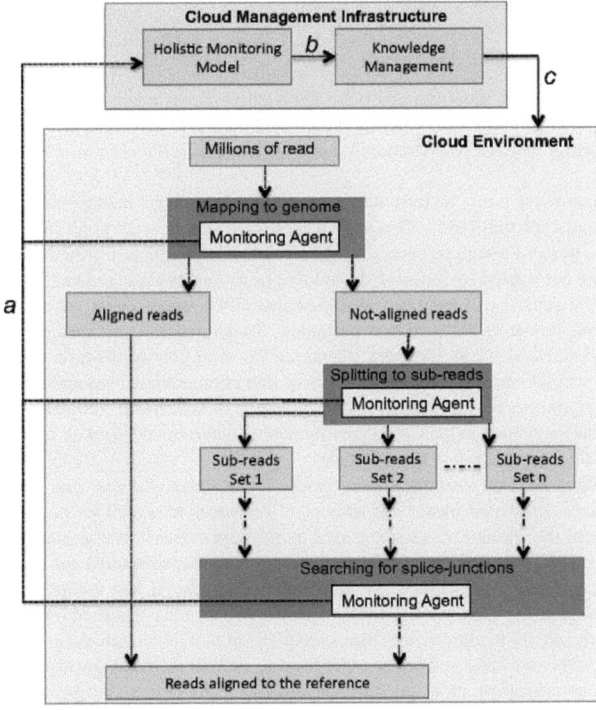

Figure 6.3: Applying Monitoring to Workflow Application

The TopHat workflow application execution is composed of different applications (sub-tasks) running sequentially and in parallel (as shown in Figure 6.2). Thus, it is necessary to monitor the computational node used to execute each of these sub-tasks in order to dynamically allocate resources if needed. As depicted in Figure 6.3, we integrate a Monitoring agent in each of these computational node used for the execution of the workflow application. The monitoring agents monitor the low-level resource metrics' status (e.g., CPU, memory, disk space, throughput, etc.) of each node and communicate the monitored information (arrow *a* in Figure 6.3) to the holistic monitoring model for processing.

57

The monitored information consists of unique IDs for each of the computational node and their resource metrics. Thus, the holistic monitoring model is capable of determining the specific node and the exact resource metric that might be lacking in the near future. It passes this information to the knowledge management component (arrow *b* in Figure 6.3) to take appropriate actions to ensure the availability of this resource for continuous execution and successful completion of the workflow (arrow *c* in Figure 6.3).

On-Demand Resource Allocation

This section describes how we apply the knowledge management techniques to allocate resources on-demand based on the monitored information. The aims of applying these techniques are to efficiently manage computational resources to support the execution of the workflow application.

To achieve these aims, we introduce a speculative knowledge management technique utilizing rule-based approach [133]. This approach ensures that at every point in time the computational nodes posses enough resources for the workflow application. Furthermore, it ensures that resources are not wasted by reducing the amount of resources allocated to a node, if necessary.

In the life sciences, it has been identified that CPU, storage, and memory are the crucial computational resources for workflow execution. To demonstrate our speculative approach, we utilize the defined SLAs in Table 6.1 to enforce the workflow application performance goals. The SLA specifies objective values for the required computational resources. Enforcing these objectives guarantees the application performance and its successful completion. The initial size of a computational node in the Cloud environment is determined based on the predefined SLAs of the workflow application to be executed.

In a further step, we introduce three notions for resource management: *allocated, utilized,* and *specified* – *allocated* means the amount of resources allocated to a computational node, *utilized* means the amount of resources used by the application executing on the computational node, and *specified* means the assumed amount of resources required for successful completion of the workflow application. An *SLA violation* occurs, if less resource is allocated than the application utilizes (or wants to utilize) with respect to the specified objective in the SLA. Consequently, we try to allocate less than specified, but more than utilized in order to avoid SLA violations on the one hand and on the other hand to prevent resource wastage.

We define allocating more or less than utilized to be called *over-provisioning* or *under-provisioning*, respectively. In order to know whether a resource r is in danger of being under-provisioned or is already under-provisioned, or whether it is over-provisioned, we calculate the current utilization $ut^r = \frac{use^r}{pr^r} \times 100$, where use^r and pr^r signify how much of a resource r was used and allocated, respectively, and divide the percentage range into three regions using Threat Thresholds (TT). In this case we define two threat thresholds TT^r_{low} and TT^r_{high} representing the higher and the lower boundaries as shown in Figure 6.4:

- Region -1: Danger of under-provisioning, or under-provisioning ($> TT^r_{high}$)
- Region 0: Well provisioned ($\leq TT^r_{high}$ and $\geq TT^r_{low}$)
- Region $+1$: Over-Provisioning ($< TT^r_{low}$)

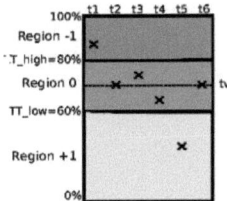

Figure 6.4: Example Behaviour of Actions at Time Intervals t1-t6

The idea of this rule-based design is to maintain an ideal value that we call *target value* $tv(r)$ for the utilization of a resource r, in exactly the centre of region 0. So, if the utilization value after some measurement leaves this region by using more (Region -1) or less resources (Region +1), then we reset the utilization to the target value, i.e., we increase or decrease allocated resources so that the utilization is again at region 0 using Equation 6.1.

$$tv(r) = \frac{TT_{low}^r + TT_{high}^r}{2}\%. \tag{6.1}$$

As long as the utilization value stays in region 0, no action is required to be executed. E.g., for $r = $ storage, $TT_{low}^r = 60\%$, and $TT_{high}^r = 80\%$, the target value would be $tv(r) = 70\%$. Figure 6.4 presents the regions and measurements (expressed as utilization of a certain resource) at time steps $t_1, t_2, \ldots, t_6$. At t_1 the utilization of the resource is in Region -1, because it is in danger of a violation. Thus, the knowledge database recommends to increase the resource such that at the next iteration t_2 the utilization is at the center of Region 0, that is, the target value. At time steps t_3 and t_4 utilization stays in the center region 0 and consequently, no action is required. At t_5, the resource is under-utilized and so the knowledge database recommends the decrease of the resource to $tv(r)$, which is attained at t_6. A large enough span between the thresholds TT_{low}^r and TT_{high}^r helps to prevent oscillations of repeatedly increasing and decreasing the same resource.

Based on these techniques, we can efficiently manage Cloud resources to provision scientific data analysis processes with enough resources to achieve high performance and to ensure their successful completion. In Section 7.6, we present the evaluations of this case study.

CHAPTER 7

Evaluation

In this chapter, we present the evaluations of our contributions, which address the challenges listed in this thesis. The evaluations are described in different sections corresponding to the framework and architectures presented in the earlier chapters.

7.1 Metrics Monitoring and Mapping Evaluation

We carried out stress tests and performance evaluations as a proof of concept for the LoM2HiS framework described in Section 3.1.

Environmental Setup

Figure 7.1 presents our designed evaluation testbed.

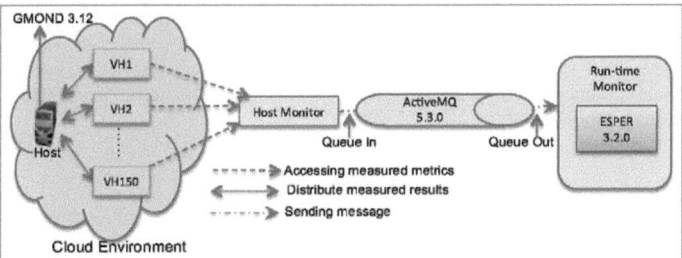

Figure 7.1: LoM2HiS Evaluation Testbed.

The aim of the presented testbed is to test the scalability and performance of the communication model and to produce a proof of concept for the *LoM2HiS* framework. Our evaluation testbed considers one physical host where *GMOND version 3.1.2* is embedded for measuring the resource metric values. From this host we simulate up to 150 virtual hosts. The virtual hosts are simulated with Java threads. Each of the threads becomes a copy of the measured raw metrics from *GMOND*. The host monitor is a Java class running on a different thread. It accesses the measured raw metrics from the virtual host threads, extracts them from their XML files and transmits them as messages (via *Queue In*) into the communication model. The essence of using many virtual hosts is to test the efficiency of the host monitor to process inputs from large number of hosts. This is equivalent to a real environment where the host monitor processes the measured metric-value pairs from different hosts.

In the evaluation of the run-time monitor, we defined an SLA agreement for an online web shop as shown in Table 7.1. The SLA parameter objective values in the table show the quality of service required by the web shop. Furthermore, in Table 7.1 we defined the threat threshold values that guide the enforcement of these SLAs. The used test system consists of an Intel Pentium Core 2 Duo 2.26 GHz, 4GB DDR3 memory, and 3Mb L2 Cache. Mac OS X 10.5 Leopard is the installed operating system and parallel desktop 4.0 is the installed virtualization environment.

Evaluation Results

This section presents the achieved results of the performance test for the host monitor, communication model, and the run-time monitor components.

Host Monitor and Communication Model Evaluation Results

Figure 7.2 presents the evaluation settings and the evaluation results of the host monitor and the communication model. In the evaluation settings, we define four experimental scenarios that are made up of numerous hosts generating large numbers of messages. Each scenario uses one defined queue. As shown in Figure 7.2, the *y-axis* represents time values and *x-axis* represents the number of hosts used, and the number of messages generated and sent through the communication model. The host monitor performance (H_{perf}) is determined considering the three internal functions responsible for: i) measuring the infrastructure resource metrics ($T_{measure}$), ii) extracting and aggregating the measured metric values ($T_{process}$), and iii) sending the extracted metric values into the communication model (T_{send}). The overall performance result is then given by Equation 7.1.

$$H_{perf} = T_{measure} + T_{process} + T_{send} \quad (7.1)$$

The communication model performance is equal to the average execution time of the underlying queue (T_{queue}).

From the results presented in Figure 7.2, it can be noticed in the four scenarios that the host monitor spends most of its time measuring the infrastructure metrics. This shows that this function is critical for the overall performance of the host monitor and should be the point of concentration in any further developments. The achieved results by the communication model for the different scenarios are relatively stable compared to the number of messages processed.

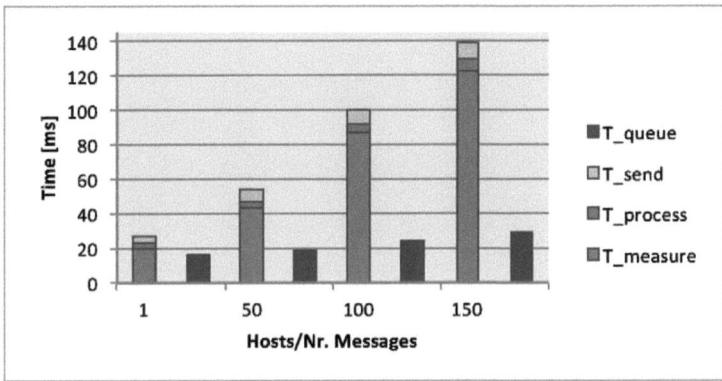

Figure 7.2: Host Monitor and Communication Model Results.

Run-Time Monitor Evaluation Results

As already discussed in Section 7.1, the evaluation of the run-time monitor is based on the settings presented in Table 7.1.

Table 7.1: Run-Time Monitor Evaluation Settings.

SLA Parameter	SLA Objective	Threat Threshold
Availability	98 %	98.9 %
Response Time	500 ms	498.9 ms
Storage	100 GB	102 GB
Memory	3 GB	3.9 GB
Incoming Bandwidth	100 Mbit/s	102 Mbit/s
Outgoing Bandwidth	50 Mbit/s	52 Mbit/s

The purpose of this evaluation is to test the overall performance of the run-time monitor. Figure 7.3 depicts the achieved performance result. The *y-axis* represents time values and the *x-axis* the number of hosts. The results are derived from the performances of its core functions responsible for: i) receiving metric-value pairs, passing them into *ESPER* engine, and querying *ESPER* (T_{rec}), ii) extracting the stored SLA from the agreed SLA repository ($T_{process}$), iii) applying mappings of low-level metrics to high-level SLA parameters (T_{map}), and iv) monitoring and enforcing agreed SLA objective for services ($T_{monitor}$). The overall run-time monitor performance (TR_{perf}) is calculated by the Equation 7.2.

$$TR_{perf} = T_{rec} + T_{process} + T_{map} + T_{monitor} \qquad (7.2)$$

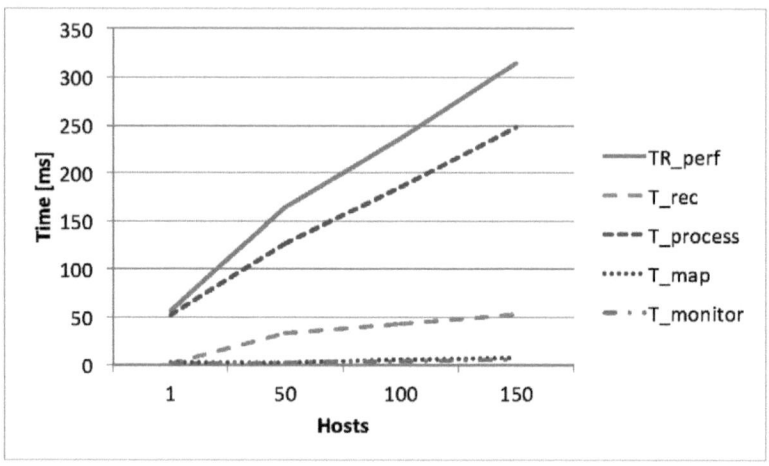

Figure 7.3: Run-Time Monitor Results.

According to the results presented in Figure 7.3 the run-time monitor's overall performance depends highly on the performance of the function to extract the agreed SLA parameters from the SLA repository ($T_{process}$). This problem can be addressed by using decentralized SLA repositories that make them local and fast accessible to each run-time monitor instance monitoring a specific service SLA.

In general, the results show that the LoM2HiS framework is scalable and could perform well in large scale Cloud environment.

7.2 Traffic Management System Monitoring Evaluation

This section presents the evaluation results of the LoM2HiS framework adopted to address the demands of traffic management systems. The goals of the evaluation are to show the scalability of the monitoring framework by means of i) the number of nodes connected to a monitoring gateway and ii) the rate by which the Lom2HiS framework requests metrics from the monitoring agents or the monitoring gateways.

The evaluation is done through simulations as presented in [172] whereby, we target the following two questions: i) How many nodes could be handled by a single monitoring gateway with a reasonable impact on network load and performance of the LCU? and ii) How often is the LoM2HiS framework allowed to retrieve metric information from a single monitoring gateway or monitoring agent with acceptable impact on the network load?

In our test-system, the impact on the traffic on the network (level 2 in Figure 7.4) and the performance of the node hosting the monitoring gateway software (level 3 in Figure 7.4) is shown by changing the parameters: i) number of hosts; and ii) frequency of retrieval.

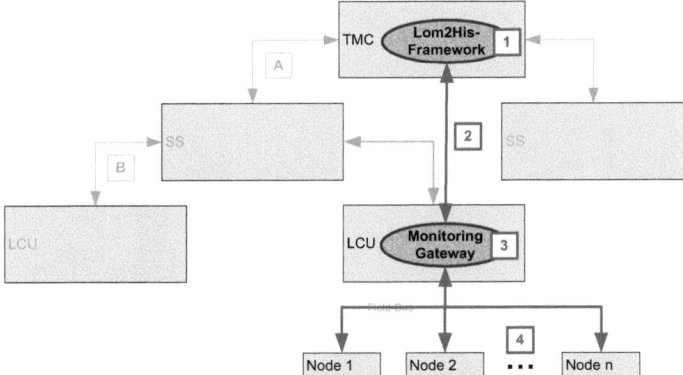

Figure 7.4: Traffic Management Evaluation Testbed.

An overview of the testbed is presented in Figure 7.4. It consists of a node simulating the TMC that hosts the LoM2HiS framework (level 1 in Figure 7.4). The node is made up of an Intel Pentium 4 Dual-core with 2.8 GHz and 2 GB of RAM. Its operating system is OpenSUSE 11.3. The host used for simulating the LCU-node (level 3) hosting the monitoring gateway is made up of a 2 GHz AMD Turion 64 X2 Mobile processor with 2 GB of RAM. Its operating system is MS-Windows XP Professional SP3.

Considering the fact that the main focus of the simulations is on the impact of running the monitoring system on an existing TMS infrastructure, the performance of the node hosting the LoM2HiS framework (i.e., the TMC) is not further considered in this work. Furthermore, the simulation does not consider traffic of "horizontal communication" between monitoring agents for backup reasons.

Communication Results

Figure 7.5 shows the evaluation results of the communication between the LoM2HiS framework and the monitoring gateway. The x-axis represents the number of hosts and the y-axis the average network traffic in Mbit/sec. The bars colored blue, red and green indicate different frequencies of retrieval, that is how often the framework retrieves the metric data from the monitoring gateway. The blue color indicates a request every second, the red color for every 10 seconds, and the green color for every 30 seconds.

According to the results in Figure 7.5, it can be noticed that the transmission of data for 100 hosts takes approximately 15–20 times the bandwidth of information for one host independent of the frequency of retrieval. This generally means, the monitored data of many hosts packed in one output XML document is transferred more efficiently than sending them in single documents. It is obvious, that the required bandwidth is directly related to the frequency of retrieval, i.e., 30

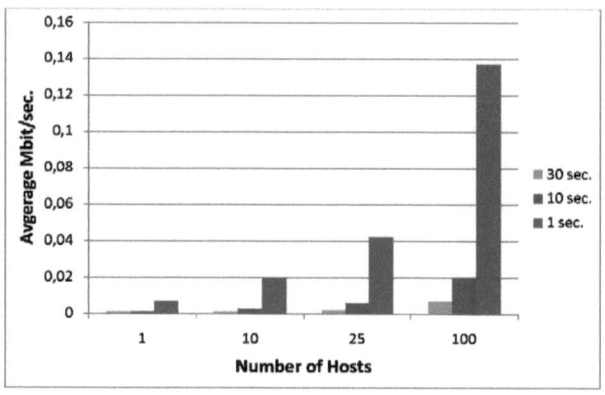

Figure 7.5: LoM2HiS Communication Evaluation Result.

retrievals each second result in 30 times the bandwidth required and therefore, have no further impact on our considerations. It is more interesting to note that a retrieval interval of one second already results in a notable bandwidth consumption. Consequently a system with 10 LCUs leads to a total bandwidth consumption of about 1.2 Mbit/s which is equal to a load of 12% in a 100 MBit network (not considering overheads).

We conclude that it is more efficient to incorporate the monitored information of as many host as possible into one XML document for transport through the network while keeping the frequency of information retrieval at an appropriate level. A 30 seconds interval still leads to an accuracy of 99.999905% over a reporting-period of 1 year which shall be sufficient for most use cases. However, in case higher resolution is needed, extensions to the metric packing strategy would be necessary.

Monitoring Gateway Performance Results

In Figure 7.6, we show the evaluation results of the time consumed on the LCU in the course of preparing the metric-data and sending them to the TMC. The preparation of data includes feeding the metrics of each node into the XML document that is in turn sent over the TCP-connection to the LoM2HiS framework on the TMC-node. The status retrieval from each node (i.e., sensors and actuators) is not considered as the data, and is assumed to be constantly fed into the metric node variables (level 4 in Figure 7.4) when communication on the field-bus occurs. The x-axis have the same meaning as in Figure 7.5, but the y-axis represents the time consumed for data preparation.

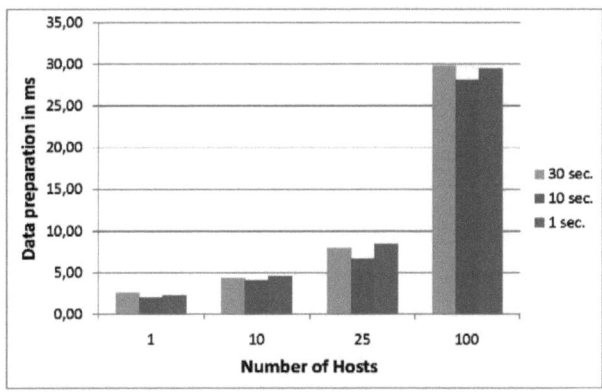

Figure 7.6: Monitoring-Gateway Performance Evaluation Result.

The results presented in Figure 7.6 indicate that the time consumed for preparation of metric-data is independent of the frequency of retrieval. The important fact to note is that the preparation of the XML document has direct impact on the time for measurement while preparation of the byte-stream and sending the data over the TCP-channel is negligible. However, preparing the XML data for more nodes at once is generally more time-efficient.

7.3 Resource and SLA Monitoring Evaluation

This section discusses the evaluation of the DeSVi architecture described in Section 3.5 using two use-case scenarios. The use-case scenarios represent the most dominant application domains provisioned in Clouds today, namely (i) high performance computing applications, which include image processing and scientific simulations; and (ii) transactional applications, which include web applications, social network sites, and media sites. The first use-case scenario comprises three types of ray-tracing applications based on POV-Ray, and the second one comprises executions of TPC-W, which is a well-known web application benchmark that simulates a web server for on-line shopping. The goal of our evaluation is to determine the efficiency of the proposed architecture in detecting SLA violations at runtime and, based on its output, suggest optimal measurement intervals for monitoring applications considering the application resource consumption behaviour.

In the following sections, we describe the experimental environment setup. Next, we present the definition of a cost function, which is used to analyze the achieved results of the two use-case scenarios. Finally, we discuss in separate sections the two experimental use-case scenarios including their achieved results and the analysis of the results.

Experimental Environment

The capacities of our private real Cloud experimental testbed is shown in Table 7.2. The table shows the resource capacities of the physical and the virtual machines being used in the experimental testbed. We use Xen virtualization technology in the testbed, precisely, we run Xen 3.4.0 on top of Oracle Virtual Machine (OVM) server.

Table 7.2: Cloud Environment Resource Setup Composed of 36 Virtual Machines.

Machine Type = Physical Machine				
OS	CPU	Cores	Memory	Storage
OVM Server	AMD Opteron 2 GHz	2	8 GB	250 GB
Machine Type = Virtual Machine				
OS	CPU	Cores	Memory	Storage
Linux/Ubuntu	AMD Opteron 2 GHz	1	1024 MB	5 GB

We have in total nine physical machines and, based on the resource capacities presented in Table 7.2, we host four VMs on each physical machine. The automated emulation framework deploys the VMs onto the physical hosts, thus creating a virtualized Cloud environment with up to 36 computing nodes capable of provisioning resources to applications. We reserve one front-end node, which is responsible for the management activities.

The front-end node serves as the control entity. It runs the automated emulation framework, the application deployer, and the LoM2HiS framework, which are the core components of the DeSVi architecture. The first two components are the supporting blocks of the experiments, whereas the third is the main component responsible for the results obtained in this section. Nevertheless, their integration is required in order to enable the experiments. Our private Cloud testbed is located at the High Performance Computing Lab at Catholic University of Rio Grande do Sul (LAD-PUCRS) Brazil. We use this virtualized environment to evaluate the two use-case scenarios presented in two later sections.

Cost Function Definition

To determine an optimal measurement interval for detecting applications' SLA objective violations at runtime, we suggest the following two determining factors i) cost of making measurements; and ii) the cost of missing SLA violations. The acceptable trade-off between these two factors defines the optimal measurement interval.

Using these two factors and other parameters, we define a cost function (C) based on which we can derive an optimal measurement interval. The ideas of defining this cost functions are derived from utility functions discussed by Lee *et al.* [115]. Equation 7.3 presents the cost function.

$$C = \mu * C_m + \sum_{\psi \in \{cpu, memory, storage\}} \alpha(\psi) * C_v \qquad (7.3)$$

where μ is the number of measurements, C_m is the cost of measurement, $\alpha(\psi)$ is the number of undetected SLA violations, and C_v is the cost of missing an SLA violation. The number of undetected SLA violations are determined based on the results of the reference measurement interval, which is assumed to be an interval capturing all the violations of an application SLA objectives.

This cost function now forms the basis for analyzing the achieved results of our two use-case scenarios in the later sections. Regarding the values of the two determining factors, we explain for each use-case scenario how we obtained these cost values.

Image Rendering Application Use-Case

We developed image rendering applications, based on the Persistence of Vision Raytracer (POV-Ray), which is a ray tracing program available for several computing platforms. In order to achieve heterogeneous load in this use-case scenario, we experiment with three POV-Ray workloads, each one with a different characteristic of time for rendering frames, as described below and illustrated in Figures 7.7 and 7.8:

- **Fish:** rotation of a fish on water. Time for rendering frames is variable.

- **Box:** approximation of a camera to an open box with objects inside. Time for rendering frames increases during execution.

- **Vase:** rotation of a vase with mirrors around. Time for processing different frames is constant.

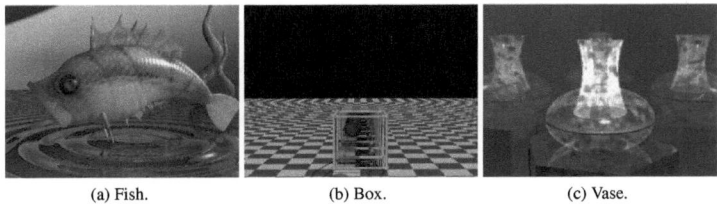

(a) Fish.   (b) Box.   (c) Vase.

Figure 7.7: Example of Images for Each of the Three Animations.

Three SLA documents are specified for the three POV-Ray applications. The SLA documents specify the level of Quality of Service (QoS) that should be guaranteed for each application during its execution. Table 7.3 presents the SLA objective thresholds for each of the

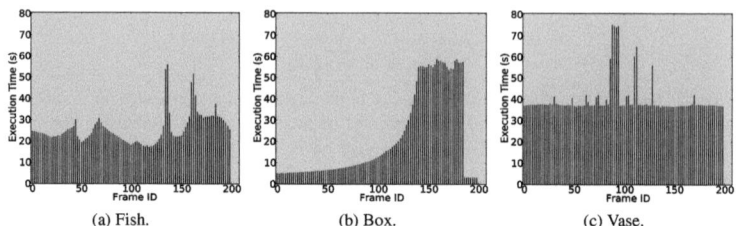

(a) Fish. (b) Box. (c) Vase.

Figure 7.8: Behaviour of Execution Time for Each POV-Ray Application.

applications. It should be noted that we are not addressing the issues of SLA definition and formalization, rather we specify SLA parameters relevant to the Cloud provider in order to manage the users' applications. These SLA objective thresholds are defined based on historical data and experiences with these specific type of applications in terms of resource consumption [160]. With the historical data, the Cloud provider can determine the amount and type of resources the application requires. Thus, the provider can make better resource provisioning plan for the applications.

Based on these SLA objective thresholds, the applications are monitored to detect SLA violations. These violations may happen either because of unforeseen resource consumptions or because SLAs are negotiated per application and not per allocated VM considering the fact that the service provider may provision different application requests on the same VM.

Table 7.3: SLA Objective Thresholds for the Three POV-Ray Applications.

SLA Parameter	Fish	Box	Vase
CPU	98.5 %	97.5 %	99.3 %
Memory	1.28 GB	1.32 GB	1.31GB
Storage	2.16 GB	2.169 GB	2.157 GB

Figure 7.9 presents the evaluation configurations for the POV-Ray applications. We instantiate 36 virtual machines that execute POV-Ray frames submitted via Application Deployer. The virtual machines are continuously monitored by Gmond. Thus, LoM2HiS has access to resource utilizations during the execution of the applications. Similarly, information about the time taken to render each frame in each virtual machine is also available to the LoM2HiS framework. These information are generated by the applications themselves and are sent to a location where the LoM2HiS can read them. As described in Figure 7.9, users supply the QoS requirements in terms of SLOs (step 1 in Figure 7.9). At the same time the images with the POV-Ray applications and input data (frames) can be uploaded to the front-end node. Based on the current system status, SLA negotiator establishes an SLA with the user. Description of the negotiation process and components is out of scope of this paper and is discussed by Brandic *et al.* [23]. Thereafter,

VM deployer starts configuration and allocation of the required VMs whereas application deployer maps the tasks to the appropriate VMs (step 3). In step 4, the application execution is triggered.

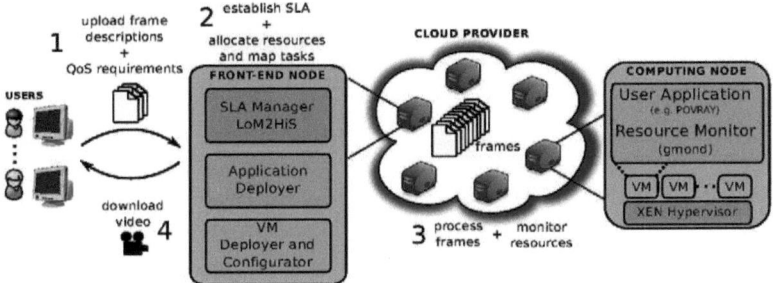

Figure 7.9: Pov-Ray Evaluation Configuration.

Image Rendering Application Use-Case Results

We defined and used seven measurement intervals to monitor the POV-Ray applications during their executions. Table 7.4 shows the measurement intervals and the number of measurements made in each interval. The applications run for about 30 minutes for each measurement interval.

Table 7.4: Measurement Intervals.

Intervals	10s	15s	20s	25s	30s	60s	120s
Nr. of Measurements	180	120	90	72	60	30	15

The 10 seconds measurement interval is a reference interval meaning the current interval used by the provider to monitor application executions on the Cloud resources. Its results show the present situation of the Cloud provider.

Figure 7.10 presents the achieved results of the three POV-Ray applications with varying characteristics in terms of frame rendering as explained earlier in this section. We use the 36 virtual machines in our testbed to simultaneously execute the POV-Ray frames. The load-balancer integrated in the application deployer ensures that the frame executions are balanced among the virtual machines.

The *LoM2HiS* framework monitors the resource usage of each virtual machine to determine if the SLA objectives are met and reports violations otherwise. Since the load-balancer balances the execution of frames among the virtual machines, we plot in Figure 7.10 the average numbers of violations encountered in the testbed for each application with each measurement interval. We analyze and interpret these results in the next section.

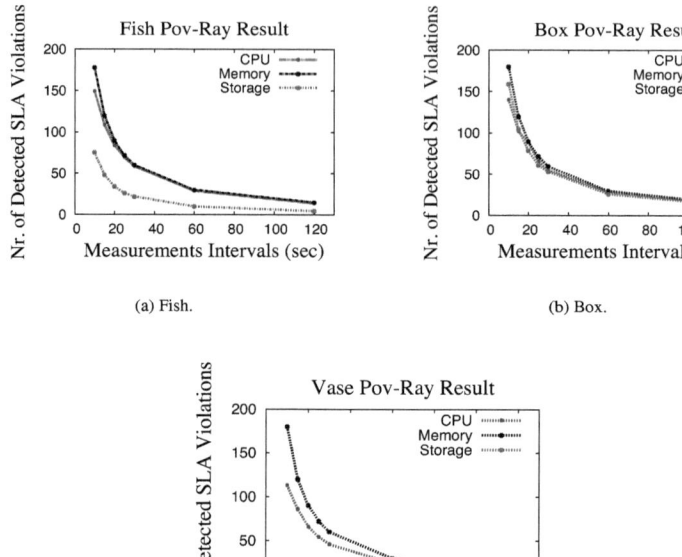

Figure 7.10: POV-Ray Experimentation Results.

Image Rendering Application Use-Case Results Analysis

The POV-Ray results presented in Figure 7.10 show that as the measurement interval increases, the number of detected SLA violation decreases. This effect is straightforward because with larger measurement intervals, the system misses detection of some SLA violations. The figures also reflect the resource consumption behaviour of the POV-Ray applications.

We carried out an intrusiveness test in our testbed to find out the processing overhead of a measurement. This determines the cost of taking measurements. The Measurement processing includes monitoring of all the virtual machines, processing of monitored data, mapping of low-level metrics to high-level SLA, and the evaluation of SLA objectives. Figure 7.11 presents the achieved result.

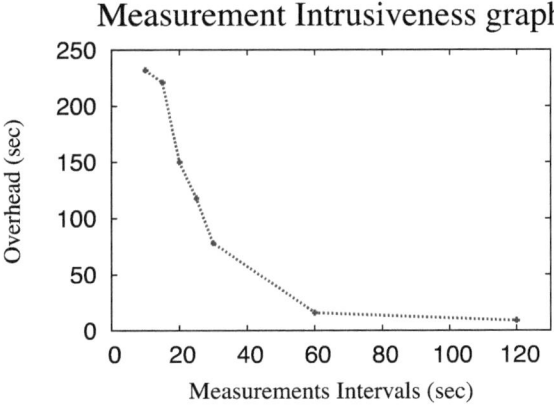

Figure 7.11: Intrusiveness Test Results.

Figure 7.11 shows the amount of overhead found in the system and how they decrease as the measurement intervals increases. This means high cost for measurements with small intervals and low cost for measurement with larger intervals.

The cost of missing SLA violation detection is an economic factor, which depends on the SLA penalty cost agreed for the specific application and the effects the violations might have on the provider for example in terms of reputation or trust issues.

By applying the cost function presented in Equation 7.3 to the achieved results of Figure 7.10, with a measurement cost of $0.6 and missing violation cost of $0.25, we achieve the monitoring costs presented in Figure 7.12. These cost values are example values for our experimental setup. They neither represents nor suggests any standard values. The approach used here is derived from the cost function approaches presented in literature [114, 194].

It should be noted in interpreting the results of Figure 7.12 that the reference measurement interval is assumed to capture all SLA violations for each application, thus it only incurs measurement cost. From the figures, it can be noticed on the one hand that the lower the frequency of measurements, the smaller the measurement cost and on the other hand, the higher the number of undetected SLA violations, the higher the cost of missing violations. This implies that to keep the detection cost low, the number of undetected SLA violations must be low.

Considering the total cost of monitoring the fish POV-Ray application in Figure 7.12a, it can be seen that the reference measurement is not the cheapest although it does not incur any cost of

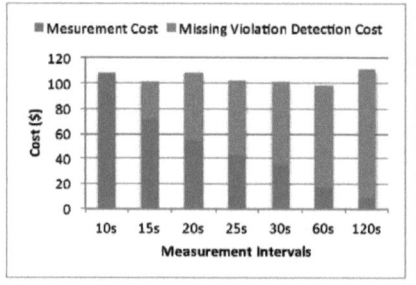
(a) Fish.

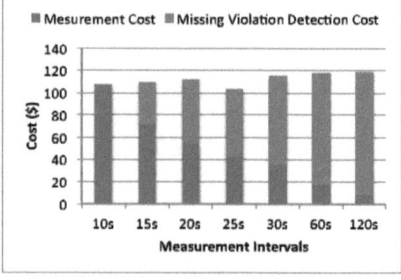
(b) Box.

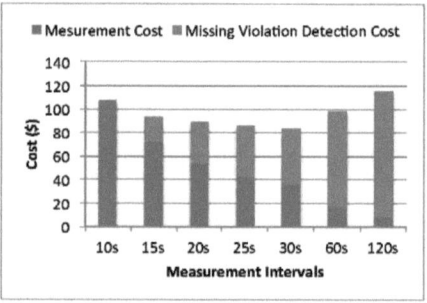
(c) Vase.

Figure 7.12: POV-Ray Application Monitoring Cost Relations.

missing SLA violation detection. In this case the 60-second interval is the cheapest and in our opinion the most suited measurement interval for this application. In the case of box POV-Ray application the total cost of monitoring, as depicted graphically in Figure 7.12b, indicates that the lowest cost is incurred with the 25-second measurement interval. Thus we conclude that this interval is best suited for this application. Also from Figure 7.12c, it is clear that the reference measurement by far is not the optimal measurement interval for the vase POV-Ray application. Thus, from the experiments the 30-second measurement interval is considered best suited for this application group.

Based on our experiments, it is observed that there is no single best suited measurement interval for all applications. Depending on how steady the resource consumption is, the monitoring infrastructure requires different measurement intervals. Notwithstanding, definition of these intervals is important to allow estimation of the impact of missed violations in applications. Note that the architecture can be configured to work with different intervals. In this case, specification of the measurement frequencies depends on policies agreed by customer and Cloud providers.

Web Application Use-Case

As a web application, we performed experiments using the Java implementation[1] of the TPC-W Benchmark [137]. This application simulates the activities of a business oriented transactional web server. The workload used in the server exercises system components related to several issues commonly found in web environments, such as multiple on-line browser sessions, dynamic page generation with database access and update, transaction integrity, and simultaneous execution of multiple transaction types.

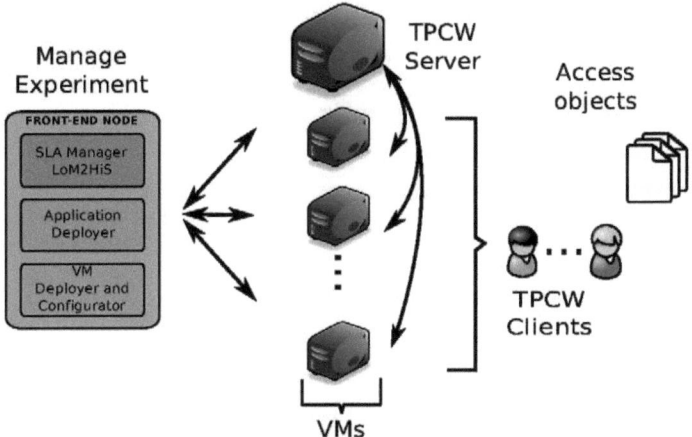

Figure 7.13: Web Application Evaluation Configuration.

We configured TPC-W to run on the 36 VMs in our setup environment. One VM is used as the server and the other 35 VMs are used as clients as shown in Figure 7.13. The clients generate requests that are handled by the server. We use the LoM2HiS framework to monitor the server and to detect SLA violations.

The quality of service requirement of the web application depends on the amount of available CPU and memory resources. Thus, we define two SLA objectives for these resource parameters to ensure the performance of the application during its execution. The values of the SLA objectives are learned based on historical data and sample runs to examine the behaviour of the application in terms of resource consumptions. For the CPU, we set a 10% threshold and for memory we set a 12% threshold. The rise of the resource utilization above these thresholds indicates an SLA violation situation.

---

[1] http://tpcw.deadpixel.de/

Web Application Use-Case Results

The resource usage of the web application server in processing the requests generated by the clients is monitored by the LoM2HiS framework in order to detect and report the SLA violations. Like in the case of POV-Ray application, we experiment here with five measurement intervals to monitor the SLAs during the application executions. The web application is allowed to run for a total length of seven minutes. In this case, small measurement intervals are chosen considering the fact that web applications' behaviour can change drastically within a period of seconds. Table 7.5 presents the achieved results.

Table 7.5: TPCW Experimentation Results.

Intervals	5s	10s	15s	20s	30s
Nr. of Measurements	84	42	28	21	14
Nr. of CPU violations detected	77	26	14	12	7
Nr. of Memory violations detected	75	41	26	19	12

Table 7.5 shows the number of measurements made with each interval and the number of SLA violations detected for the CPU and memory resources. Based on these results, we apply the cost function in the next section to analyze and determine the optimal measurement interval.

Web Application Use-Case Results Analysis

As presented in Table 7.5, the number of SLA violations detected decreases as the measurement interval frequency grows. This is an expected logical behaviour. Therefore, to find the optimal measurement interval we apply the cost function of Equation 7.3 on the achieved results.

In this use-case scenario, the cost of measurement is low considering the experimental setup shown in Figure 7.13. With the setup, the processing of client requests are performed on the TPC-W server, thus only this server is monitored to detect SLA violations. Therefore, there is a low overhead in monitoring this single machine. On the other side, the cost of missing SLA violation is high because the web application performance degrades very fast once the SLA objectives are violated, which can frustrate a customer waiting for a response of the application. e.g., waiting for a browser to load.

On the basis that the cost of measurement is low and the cost of missing SLA violation detection is high, we use $0.15 as the measurement cost and $0.30 as the cost of missing violation. Note that the 5s measurement interval is a reference interval, which means that it detects all SLA violation and acts as the current default measurement interval. Thus, it incurs only measurement cost and no cost for missing SLA violation detection. Applying these values to the cost function, we achieve the results depicted in Figure 7.14.

The results show the total cost incurred by each of the measurement intervals. The cost of missing SLA violation detection increases as the measurement interval frequency decreases. This is caused by the fact that the larger the measurement interval, the lower the number of

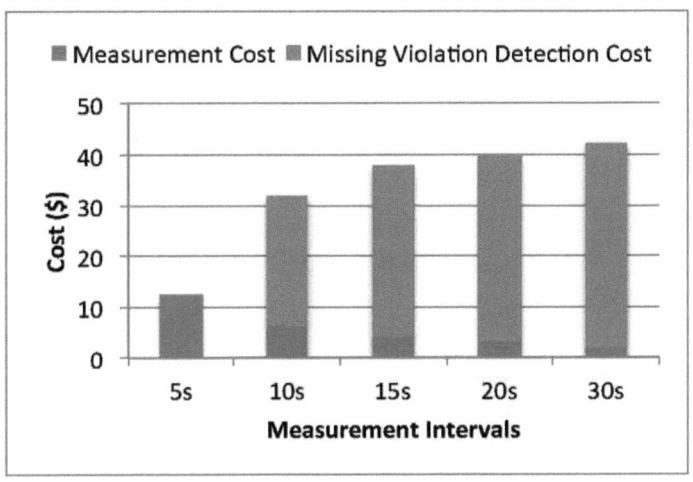

Figure 7.14: Web Application Cost Relations.

measurements made and the higher the number of missed SLA violations. Failure to detect SLA violations means costly SLA penalties for the provider and poor performance of the application.

Therefore, from our experiments we could not find a larger, better measurement interval than the 5 seconds reference measurement interval, what confirms our assumptions that web applications are highly sensitive and should be monitored at small intervals to ensure their quality of service. Furthermore, there can be a surge in clients request of a web application within short periods of time, thus the monitoring mechanism should be able to detect such situations.

The whole set of experiments presented in this section clearly demonstrate the need for fine-tuning of monitoring systems to the specific requirements of Cloud applications. However, different applications have needs for different measurement intervals, and even though some applications are more stable than other in terms of resource requirements, defining automatic methods for finding the optimal measurement interval of each application is a non-trivial problem, which we addressed with the application monitoring architecture described in Chapter 5.

7.4 SLA-Aware Scheduling Evaluation

In this section, we discuss the evaluation of the scheduling heuristic presented in Chapter 4. The evaluation demonstrates the resource utilization efficiency achievable by the scheduler. It further shows the higher application performance obtainable while compared to an arbitrary task scheduler. The evaluations presented here are realized using the CloudSim simulation tool [34].

We start with the experimental setup and configuration descriptions.

Basic Experimental configurations

The experimental testbed is setup as described in Figure 7.15. It demonstrates the processes of placing service request by customers and how our proposed scheduler deploys the service on appropriate Cloud resources.

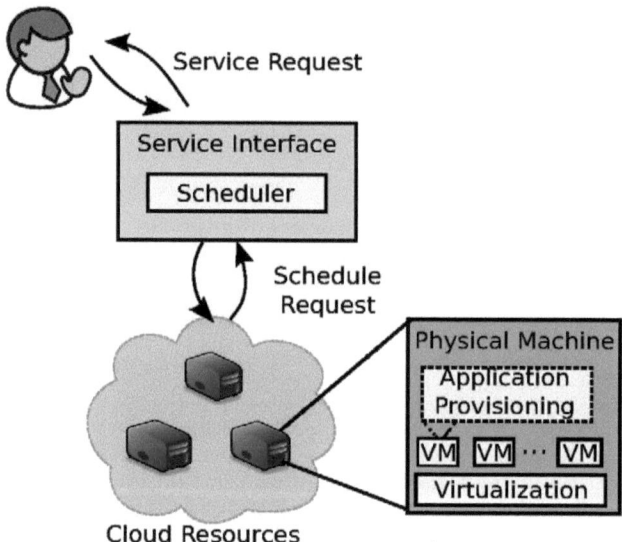

Figure 7.15: Scheduling Evaluation Testbed.

The Cloud resources comprises physical and virtual machines. Table 7.6 shows the resource capacities of the physical machines and the configuration parameters of the virtual machines. Based on the capacities of the physical machine resources and the sizes of the virtual machines, we can start several virtual machines on one physical host in the CloudSim simulation engine.

To achieve a reasonable application deployment scenario, we use two types of applications each with its own SLA terms to realize heterogeneous workloads. The first workload is extracted from a Web Application (WA) for an online shop and the second workload is a trace of High Performance Computing (HPC) application represented by an image rendering applications such as POV-Ray [2].

---

[2] www.povray.org

Table 7.6: Cloud Environment Resource Setup

Machine Type = Physical Machine					
OS	CPU Core	CPU Speed	Memory	Storage	Bandwidth
Linux	6	6000 MIPS	3.072 GB	30000 GB	3 Gbit/s
Machine Type = Virtual Machine					
OS	CPU Core	CPU Speed	Memory	Storage	Bandwidth
Linux	1	1000 MIPS	512 MB	5000 GB	500 Mbit/s

Table 7.7 presents our experimental SLA objective terms for the two application types. The web application generally requires less resources while executing and its performance is ensured by the specified SLA objectives. The HPC applications are resource intensive in execution and their performance are safeguarded by the specified SLA objectives. Guaranteeing these SLA terms ensures the good performance of the application executions.

Table 7.7: Heterogenous Application SLA Objectives

Application Type	CPU Power	Memory	Storage	Bandwidth
Web	240 MIPS	130 MB	1000 GB	150 Mbit/s
HPC	500 MIPS	250 MB	2000 GB	240 Mbit/s

Deployment Efficiency and Resource Utilization

In this experiment, we evaluate the efficiency of the proposed scheduler for deploying customer service requests and utilizing the available Cloud resources. Furthermore, we test the essence of the on-demand resource provisioning feature. We simulate a large data center made up of 60 physical machines and 370 virtual machines. We generate and use 1500 service requests for the experiment.

To evaluate the capabilities of the scheduler, we divide our evaluation into two groups: i) fixed resource and ii) on-demand resource. In the fixed resource group the on-demand resource provisioning feature is deactivated while in the on-demand resource group, it is activated. The essence of these two groups is to demonstrate the advantages of the on-demand resource provisioning feature. Each group runs three scenarios:

- The first scenario handles the deployment of *only web applications'* service requests.

- The second scenario deals *only with HPC applications.*

- The third scenario deals with a *mixture of web and HPC applications.*

The three scenarios are intended to cover real world deployment situations in the sense that they handle applications from different categories, which exhibit different behaviours in terms of resource consumption. In the scenarios, the service requests are randomly generated and sent to the scheduler for scheduling and deployment. In the next step, we describe the achieved results of these two groups.

Fixed resource group: In this case, the scheduler schedules and deploys the applications on the available running VM in the data center without the flexibility of starting new VMs when required. The results achieved by the three scenarios of this group are presented in Figure 7.16.

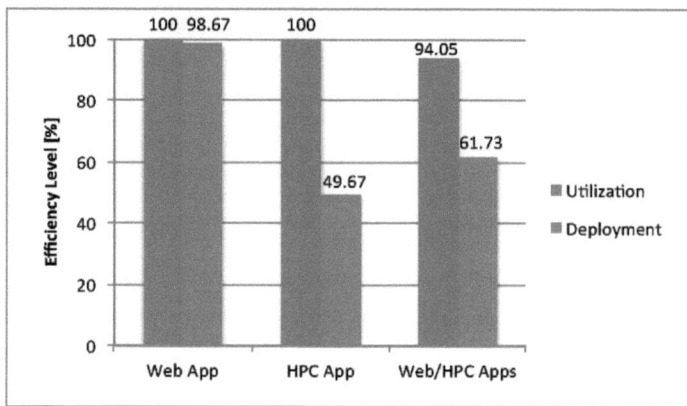

Figure 7.16: Scheduling and Deploying With Fixed Resources.

As shown in Figure 7.16, scenario 1 presents the results of the first evaluation scenario, which handles only web applications. The first bar shows the total resource utilization level achieved among the running VMs in the data center. The resource utilization is measured by checking the number of service applications the scheduler can deploy on each virtual machine in relation to the resource capacity of the virtual machine. In this scenario, the scheduler achieved 100% resource utilization meaning that the resources on each VM were adequately utilized. The second bar shows the total deployment efficiency achieved by the scheduler. The deployment efficiency is calculated by counting the total number of deployed service applications in relation to the total number of requested services. In this scenario a total of 1480 service applications are deployed whereas a total of 1500 service requests were made. This gives a deployment efficiency of 98,67%. About 20 service requests could not be provisioned due to lack of resources on the available VMs.

The results of the second evaluation scenario dealing with only HPC applications are presented as Scenario 2 in Figure 7.16. The first bar shows the resource utilization achieved by the scheduler, which is in this case 100%. That means the scheduler was able to fully utilize the resources of the available VMs. The second bar represents the deployment efficiency achieved, which is in this scenario 49.67%. The low deployment efficiency is caused by lack of available resources. Considering the heavy resource consumption of the HPC applications, they require much larger resources thereby easily consuming the available resource in the data center.

The results of the third evaluation scenario are presented as Scenario 3 in Figure 7.16. This scenario deals with a mixture of web and HPC applications' service requests. Approximately an equal number of service requests for both application types are generated. The scheduler achieved about 94.05% resource utilization in this scenario as shown by the first bar. The inability to achieve 100% resource utilization is caused by the heterogenous nature of the workload whereby some HPC applications cause some resource fragmentation leaving some resource fragments that are not usable by the scheduler. The second bar represents the deployment efficiency of this scenario, which is 61.73%. This is significantly better than the deployment efficiency achieved in the second scenario. This increase in deployment efficiency is attributed by the heterogenous workload whereby the number of HPC applications' requests is smaller than in the second scenario.

On-demand resource group: In this group, it is possible for the scheduler to flexibly start new VMs when necessary as far as there are available resources on the physical machines. This feature allows for higher service request deployment and better usage of the resources at the data center. The results obtained by the three evaluation scenarios of this group are depicted in Figure 7.17.

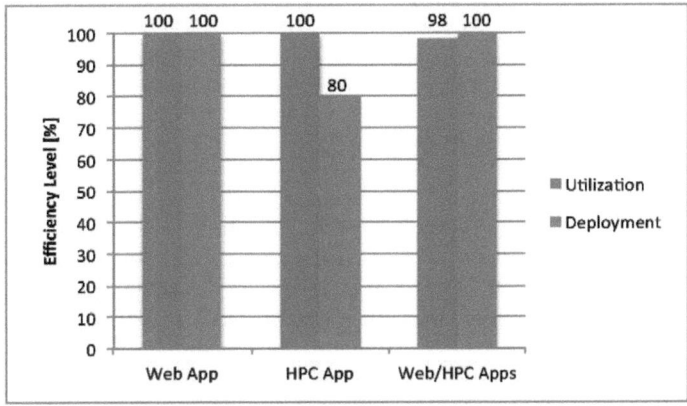

Figure 7.17: Scheduling and Deploying With On-demand Resource Provisioning Feature.

The first scenario handles only web applications. Its results are presented as Scenario 1 in Figure 7.17. The first bar shows that the scheduler achieved 100% utilization in this case. The interesting observation in this scenario compared to the first scenario of the fixed group, is the 100% deployment efficiency achieved, which is shown by the second bar. The scheduler made advantage of the flexible on-demand resource provisioning feature to start extra four virtual machines to fully deploy the whole service requests.

The second evaluation scenario results are presented as Scenario 2 in Figure 7.17. This scenario deals with only HPC applications. The scheduler achieved 100% resource utilization in scheduling and deploying the HPC applications as depicted by the first bar. That means the available resources are fully utilized. Although the resources were fully utilized, the scheduler could only achieve 80% deployment efficiency. This is a far better result than 49.67% achieved by the equivalent scenario in the fixed group. The scheduler created extra 229 VMs for the applications deployments thereby reaching the limits of the physical machines. The scheduler could not achieve 100% deployment efficiency due to an ultimate lack of resources in the data center. This problem could be addressed with Cloud federation paradigm.

Scenario 3 as shown in Figure 7.17 depicts the results of the third evaluation scenario dealing with a mixture of web and HPC applications. The scheduler achieved 98% resource utilization due to resource fragmentations caused by the heterogenous workload and resource over-provisioning. The last two VMs started on-demand were under-utilized. A 100% deployment efficiency was achieved in this scenario by starting 215 VMs on-demand.

Comparing the results achieved by the former group scenarios (Figure 7.16) against those of the later group (Figure 7.17), it can be clearly seen that the later group obtained much better resource utilization rates and deployment efficiencies. This demonstrates the effectiveness and relevance of our proposed scheduling approach in a Cloud environment.

Application Performance Comparison

In this section, we discuss the performance of the applications being provisioned in the Cloud simulation testbed. The application performance is evaluated in two aspects using the scenarios of the previous section: i) response time for the web applications and ii) completion time for the HPC applications. We compare the result achieved by our proposed scheduler with that achieved by an arbitrary task scheduler.

Table 7.8: Scheduler Comparison

	Without On-demand Resource Provisioning Feature			
	SLA-aware Scheduler		Traditional Task Scheduler	
Scenario	Response Time	Completion Time	Response Time	Completion Time
1	8sec	-	20sec	-
2	-	10sec	-	22sec
3	10sec	14sec	25sec	30sec
	With On-demand Resource Provisioning Feature			
	SLA-aware Scheduler		Traditional Task Scheduler	
Scenario	Response Time	Completion Time	Response Time	Completion Time
1	5sec	-	15sec	-
2	-	7sec	-	18sec
3	8sec	10sec	19sec	24sec

Table 7.8 presents the applications performance results. The results show the average response time and completion time of the applications while deployed by the two schedulers. It can be clearly seen that our proposed scheduler is two times better than the task scheduler. The

good performance of our scheduler is attributed to the fact that it considers multiple performance objectives before deciding on which resource to deploy an application thereby finding the optimal resource combination for the application best performance, whereas the task scheduler considers mainly single objectives in its deployment, which can not provide the optimal resources for the application best performance. Note that in Table 7.8 the on-demand resource provisioning feature applies only to our proposed scheduler.

7.5 Application Monitoring Evaluation

The primary goal of this evaluation is to provide a proof of concept for the *CASViD* application monitoring architecture presented in Chapter 5. In this regard, we evaluate two aspects: (i) the ability of the architecture to monitor applications at runtime to detect SLA violations and (ii) the capability of automatically determining the optimal measurement interval for efficient monitoring. We carry out these evaluations using real world applications provisioning scenarios executed on a real Cloud testbed and discuss the applicability of the CASViD architecture in large-scale Cloud environments. We also show results on monitoring intrusion of the CASViD monitor.

For this evaluation, we utilize the private Cloud testbed described in Section 7.3 and presented in Figure 7.9. In the next section, we discuss the utility function to determine the optimal measurement interval for application performance monitoring.

Utility Function Definition

The optimal measurement interval is an economic factor. The goals of the provider are i) to achieve the maximal profit; and ii) to maintain the agreed SLA objectives for the applications while efficiently utilizing resources. The trade-off between these two factors determines the optimal measurement interval. To derive such an interval, we define a utility function (U) for the provider, which is based on experiences gained from existing utility functions discussed by Lee *et al.* [115]. The utility function considers on the one hand the provider profit and on the other hand the cost associated with the effort of detecting SLA violations and the penalty cost of the violations. Equation 7.4 presents the utility function.

$$U = \sum_{\beta \in \{customer\}} P_c(\beta) * P_t(\beta) - (\mu * M_c + \sum_{\psi \in \{RT, TP\}} \alpha(\psi) * V_p) \qquad (7.4)$$

where P_c is the service provisioning cost, P_t is the provisioning duration in minutes, μ is the number of measurements, M_c is the measurement cost, $\alpha(\psi)$ is the number of detected SLA violations of the SLA objectives, RT is the response time, TP is the throughput, and V_p is the SLA violation penalty. $P_c * P_t$ is equal to the provider profit. Defining the service provisioning cost is subject to negotiations between the customer and the service provider. In our experiments, we defined service provisioning costs based on experiences from existing approaches [114, 194]. This utility function is not a configuration for the experimentations rather it is used to analyze the achieved results. The values of the parameters are different for each customer/application type.

Experimental Application Workload

We use variants of the POV-Ray application presented in Section 7.3 for the evaluations in this section. For the experiments, we designed three workload applications that can be executed sequentially or simultaneously on our Cloud testbed environment. With the three workloads, we cover different application behaviours thereby realizing heterogeneous load in the experiments. The workloads are based on three POV-Ray applications with different characteristics of time for rendering frames. The POV-Ray application workload used are variants of the following:

- **Fish** application workload,
- **Box** application workload, and
- **Vase** application workload.

Each workload contains approximately 2000 tasks. Each task has an execution time that varies from 10 to 40 seconds.

Our architecture handles simultaneous customer provisioning. Therefore, the experiments contain three scenarios, where each scenario has a given number of customers. These scenarios represents real world provisioning situations where a provider is simultaneously provisioning one or multiple customer applications using his Cloud resources. Furthermore, it shows the ability of the CASViD architecture to independently monitor the application performance of each customer.

Each customer has a distinct SLA document for his/her workload application. The SLAs must be guaranteed for each application to avoid costly SLA penalties. Table 7.9 presents the SLA objectives for the applications. These SLA objectives are defined based on historical data and experiences with these specific application types. The response time is expressed in seconds and the throughput in frames per second (f/s). The customer application stack to be provisioned on the Cloud environment is made up of i) the SLA document specifying the quality of service for the application and ii) the application files to be executed.

Achieved Experimental Results

We defined and used five measurement intervals to monitor the application workloads in this experiment. Table 7.10 shows the achieved results of the three scenarios for each measurement interval. The applications run for about 12 minutes in scenario 1, 22 minutes in scenario 2, and 30 minutes in scenario 3. The different execution length of the scenarios is necessary to investigate the application behaviours in each case.

The applications in scenario 2 & 3 are simultaneously executed on our Cloud testbed. The load-balancer integrated in the application deployer ensures that the application execution is distributed among the virtual machines. The SLA management framework uses the *CASViD monitor* to monitor the application metrics in order to determine if the SLA objectives are ensured and reports violations otherwise.

Table 7.10 shows the number of SLA violations detected with each measurement interval for the two SLA parameters - Response Time and Throughput. These two SLA parameters are

Table 7.9: SLA Objective Thresholds Specification.

	Scenario 1		
SLA Parameter	Customer1		
Response Time	265s		
Throughput	2.75 f/s		
	Scenario 2		
SLA Parameter	Customer1	**Customer2**	
Response Time	430s	540s	
Throughput	3.99 f/s	1.35 f/s	
	Scenario 3		
SLA Parameter	**Customer1**	**Customer2**	**Customer3**
Response Time	795s	430s	1030s
Throughput	0.965 f/s	2.31 f/s	0.709 f/s

monitored in this evaluation because they define the desirable quality of service for the POV-Ray applications. In case of different application types, the parameters to be monitored might differ.

In Table 7.10, the five seconds measurement intervals is a reference interval meaning the current interval used by the provider to monitor application executions. To explain the results in the table for example in scenario 1, the customer application provisioning length was 12 minutes. With 10 seconds interval, we made 72 measurements within this provisioning time length. With these measurements, 51 response time SLA violations and 16 throughput SLA violations were detected.

As shown in Table 7.10, the number of detected SLA violations decreases as the measurement interval increases. This is due to the missed SLA violation detection in between the measurement interval. It illustrates the risk involved with larger measurement intervals. We analyze these results in a different section to determine the optimal measurement intervals.

CASViD Monitor Intrusion

One of the issues that are typically evaluated in a monitoring system is its intrusion, i.e., what is the overhead incurred in the system when the monitoring is used. The intrusion of a monitoring system is usually related to the sampling or measurement frequency used. Higher frequencies result in a higher intrusion.

In order to evaluate the intrusion of CASViD monitor, we execute the three POV-Ray workloads (Box, Fish and Vase), measure the total execution time without monitoring, and compared against the total execution time using the monitoring system with different sampling frequencies. The sampling frequencies were 1, 2, 3, 6 and 12 samples per minute, which corresponds to 60, 30, 20, 10 and 5 seconds of interval between samples.

The chart in Figure 7.18 shows the intrusion with each workload. We can observe that the intrusion in all workloads presented a linear behaviour in relation to the sampling frequency. In all cases, the sampling frequency of 3 samples per minute (20-second interval) produced an

Table 7.10: Number of Detected SLA Violations.

		Scenario 1					
		Intervals	5s	10s	20s	30s	60s
		Nr. of Measurements	144	72	36	24	12
		Customer1		Nr. of Violations			
		Response Time	112	51	17	9	4
SLA Parameter		Throughput	54	16	4	3	1
		Scenario 2					
		Intervals	5s	10s	20s	30s	60s
		Nr. of Measurements	264	132	66	44	22
		Customer1		Nr. of Violations			
		Response Time	49	20	11	5	3
SLA Parameter		Throughput	128	54	27	16	4
		Customer2		Nr. of Violations			
		Response Time	120	93	31	19	8
SLA Parameter		Throughput	90	49	14	8	2
		Scenario 3					
		Intervals	5s	10s	20s	30s	60s
		Nr. of Measurements	360	180	90	60	30
		Customer1		Nr. of Violations			
		Response Time	165	109	39	19	9
SLA Parameter		Throughput	141	73	14	7	2
		Customer2		Nr. of Violations			
		Response Time	128	80	40	27	13
SLA Parameter		Throughput	137	92	42	26	12
		Customer3		Nr. of Violations			
		Response Time	219	167	98	24	12
SLA Parameter		Throughput	190	87	77	14	6

intrusion smaller than 1%, resulting in a small impact in the workload performance. Due to the linearity in the monitor's intrusion, the sampling frequency can be easily tuned to reach a desired intrusion boundary.

In the next section, we analyze the achieved monitored results whereby we consider the monitoring intrusiveness in defining the cost of measurement to be used in the utility function presented in Equation 7.4 for the analysis.

Results Analysis

In this section, we first manually analyze the achieved results to determine the optimal measurement interval using the utility function defined in Equation 7.4. Then, we demonstrate the

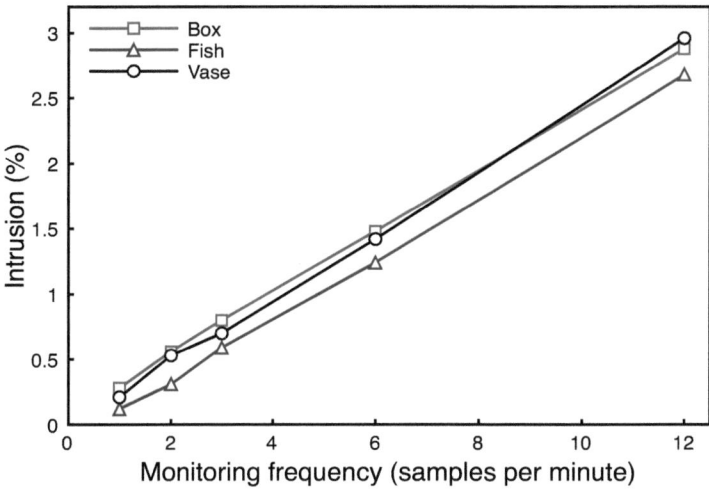

Figure 7.18: CASViD Monitor's Intrusion with Different Sampling Frequencies.

method to automatically determine this interval using Algorithm 5.1 in Section 5.2. The experimental scenarios are analyzed separately.

The first scenario (Table 7.9) deals with provisioning and monitoring of one customer application. In this case the customer pays a provisioning cost of $0.6 per minute (i.e., the service price) and the provisioning time length is 12 minutes. The SLA penalty cost is $0.04 and the cost of measurement is $0.02. Note that the cost values are experimental values. The idea is derived from existing approaches presented in literature [114, 194].

Figure 7.19 presents the analyzed results of scenario 1. The 5-second interval is the reference measurement interval to capture all SLA violations for the applications in each case.

The analyzed results show the net utility (in dollar) of the provider with each measurement interval. The net utility translates into the profit of the provider in provisioning the customer application. The 10-second measurement interval has the highest net utility and is considered the optimal one. The later intervals miss several SLA violations and thereby incur high penalty cost.

In Scenario 2, the provider provisions and monitors two customer applications using their specified SLA objectives as shown in Table 7.9. The first customer pays a provisioning cost of $0.5 per minute while the second customer pays $0.4 per minute. SLA penalty cost of $0.045 was agreed for customer 1 and $0.038 for customer 2. The measurement cost is the same for both applications and is specified to be $0.037. Applying these values in the utility function of Equation 7.4 we achieve the results presented in Figure 7.20.

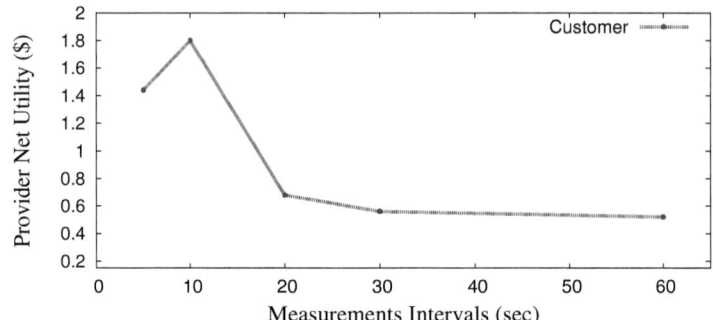

Figure 7.19: Scenario 1 Analyzed Results.

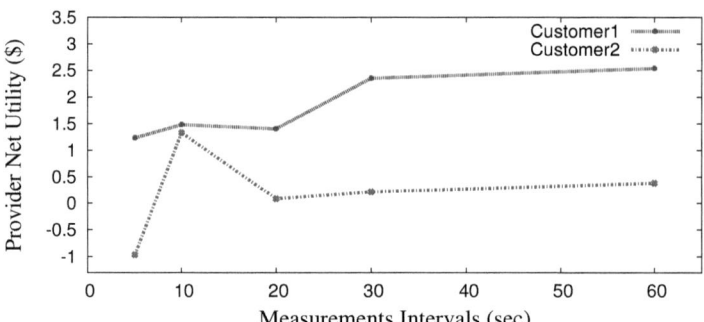

Figure 7.20: Scenario 2 Analyzed Results.

As depicted in Figure 7.20, for customer 1, the 60-second measurement interval has the highest net utility and in our opinion the optimal measurement interval for the provider to adequately monitor the application of this customer. The other intervals provide lesser utility for the provider. For customer 2, the 10-second measurements interval proves to be the optimal one with the highest net utility. In this case it can be seen that the reference measurement interval provides a negative utility meaning that the provider loses revenues in his current situation. Therefore, finding another measurement interval is essential for the business continuity of the provider.

Scenario 3 consists of the provisioning and monitoring of three different customer applications based on their respective SLA objectives. Customer 1 pays a provisioning cost of $0.5

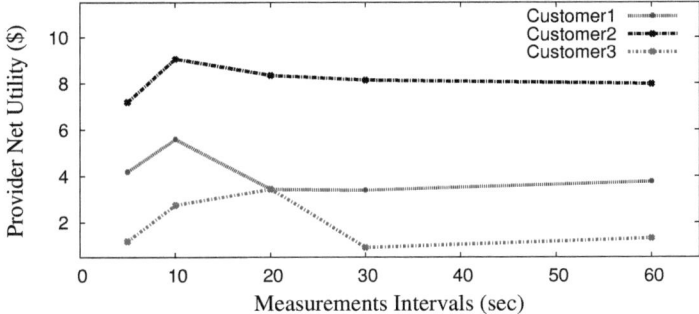

Figure 7.21: Scenario 3 Analyzed Results.

per minute and customer 2 pays $0.6 per minute while customer 3 pays $0.4 per minute. The agreed SLA penalty for customer 1 is $0.035, for customer 2 is $0.038, and for customer 3 is $0.025. The customer applications executes simultaneously on the testbed, thus there is only one measurement cost of $0.03.

Figure 7.21 presents the analyzed results of this scenario. As shown in Figure 7.21, for customer 1 and 2, the 10-second measurement interval provides the highest net utility and therefore, is the optimal interval for the provider to cost-efficiently monitor the application of these customers at runtime. In the case of customer 3, the 20-second interval provides the highest net utility and is considered the optimal measurement interval for this customer applications.

Generally, the optimal measurement interval determined by the total net utility is a tradeoff between the monitoring cost and the number of detected SLA violations at runtime (see Equation 7.4). The monitoring cost represents the efforts and overheads in monitoring the applications while the number of detected SLA violations determines the amount of penalty cost the provider has to pay to the customer. Thus, these two parameters express the efficiency and cost of monitoring an application execution.

Based on our experiments, the proposed architecture proved to be efficient in monitoring and detecting application SLA violation situations. As described in Section 5.2, the optimal measurement interval depends on the application and its input and has to be determined automatically. Figure 7.22 presents the behaviour of the provider net utility for the 10-second measurement interval over the execution of the entire application of scenario 1. This demonstrates the method to automatically find the optimal measurement interval. From the figure, it can be observed that after 5 minutes, the metric gets steady. As the net utility reaches this stability, it is possible to have a good prediction on this metric for this interval. Therefore, by doing so for other intervals, it is possible to automatically find the one that provides best cost-benefit value for measuring and detecting SLAs. The basic idea is that a user would specify a range of possible intervals (based on personal experience with the application/environment) and the monitoring architect

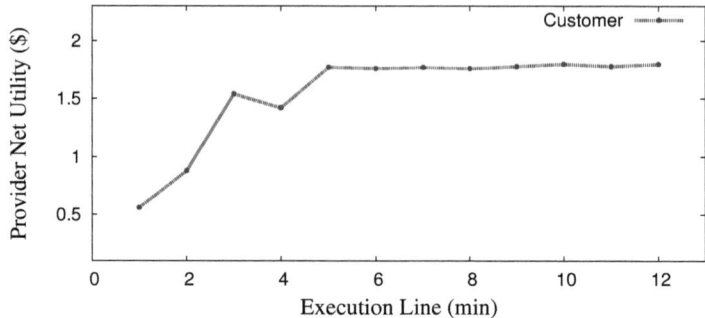

Figure 7.22: Behaviour of Provider Net Utility for the 10-sec Measurement Interval.

would detect the suitable measurement interval via Algorithm 5.1.

Applying CASViD in Large-Scale Environments

The experiments so far were performed in a real testbed for a small scenario. To apply the CASViD architecture in a large-scale Cloud environment, there are two challenges to be addressed: (i) large number of users and (ii) many application types. The issue of large number of users is not trivial for monitoring and detecting SLA violations in large-scale Clouds. This problem has been addressed with the design of our monitoring framework. The separation of the monitoring activities from the analysis of the monitored results as described in our testbed setups, where we explained the functions of the front-end node to be the entity controlling and analyzing the monitored data; and the computing node to be the entity where the application task are executed. We employ monitoring agents on the computing node to monitor the application metrics and communicate back the monitored data to the front-end node for analysis. This design strategy makes our architecture scalable and capable of usage in large-scale environments.

The efficiency of automatically determining the optimal measurement interval for many application types depends on the number of concurrent request at each period of time. This issue has been addressed with Algorithm 5.1 presented in Section 5.2. This algorithm is capable of quickly selecting appropriate measurement intervals for monitoring the provisioning of different customer application in large-scale Cloud environments.

This claim of applying CASViD in large scale environment is still in theory, we have not carried out practical evaluations.

7.6 Case Study Evaluation

In this section, we present the evaluation of the case study integrating monitoring with knowledge management as described in Section 6.3 to realize an autonomic Cloud management infrastructure. The goals of the evaluation are to show the applicability of the holistic monitoring model to monitor workflow application executions and the usage of the knowledge management techniques to efficiently manage resources to prevent SLA violations. We start with the discussion of the environmental setups.

Experimental Setup

The evaluation is carried out in a virtualized Cloud environment. The workflow application is executed using virtual machines and each of them can have its capacity increased up to the values presented in Table 7.11.

Table 7.11: Computational Node Capacity

OS	CPU	Cores	Memory	Storage
Linux/Ubuntu	Intel Xeon(R) 3 GHz	2	9 GB	19 GB

The virtual machines (VMs) represent computational nodes for the execution of the workflow applications. The VMs in our evaluation environment are created using VMWare tools. Figure 7.23 presents an overview of the evaluation testbed. The testbed represents a setup for efficient management of application execution in a Cloud environment. The purpose of the testbed is to present a proof of our concept and to demonstrate how workflow application executions could be efficiently managed in a Cloud environment.

On the testbed, one of the nodes acts as the control entity. It hosts the holistic monitoring model, the knowledge management component, and provides an interface for deploying workflow applications.

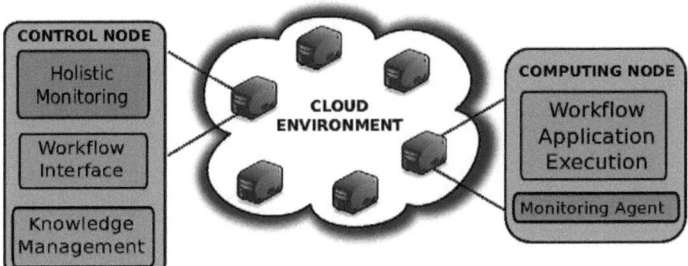

Figure 7.23: Evaluation Testbed

The evaluation of our approach is based on the bioinformatic workflow application *TopHat*, which was described in Section 6.3. It aligns RNA-Seq reads to mammalian-sized genomes using the ultra high-throughput short read aligner *Bowtie* [112], and then analyses the mapping results to identify splice junctions between exons. Furthermore, it uses the Sequence Alignment/Map (SAM) tools in its execution. SAM tools provide various utilities for manipulating alignments in the SAM format, including sorting, merging, indexing, and generating alignments in a per-position format [118].

We analysed a set of RNA-Seq data using the *TopHat* workflow application, and the achieved results are presented in the next sections.

Monitoring Results

As outlined in Section 6.3, we use the holistic monitoring model to monitor the TopHat workflow application while analyzing RNA-Seq data for the duration of three hours execution. We monitored the status of the resource metrics *CPU, memory* and *storage* at runtime with a measurement interval of one minute. The achieved results are presented in the figures below. Note that the monitored results presented are from one of the computational node and not the entire Cloud environment. The resource consumption behaviours on the different computational nodes are similar, thus, we present the results from one node for simplicity and ease of understanding our approach.

The aim of the monitoring processes is to timely detect the unavailability of computational resources. To realize this, our holistic monitoring model utilizes monitoring agents to monitor the resource status and compares them against the *threat thresholds*, which are defined values to signal the shortage of computational resources, in its monitoring operations. The threat thresholds can be dynamically or statically defined. In this approach, the knowledge management dynamically updates the initial predefined threat thresholds.

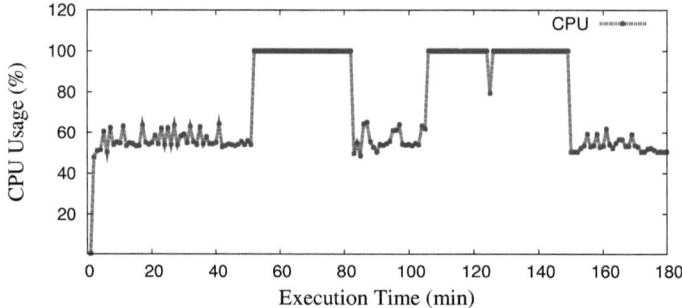

Figure 7.24: Monitored CPU Utilization

Figure 7.24 presents the monitored results for the CPU usage. From the results, it can be observed that the TopHat workflow application in some time intervals is very CPU intensive. For example from the execution time 52 to 80. These time intervals where the CPU usage is 100% are the critical ones that need to be managed. The monitoring model is configured in this case with a threat threshold value of about 80% CPU utilization. This means, once the CPU utilization exceeds this threshold, it sends a notification message to the knowledge management to provide preventive actions to avoid reaching 100% utilization, because at that point the performance of TopHat degrades and there might be risk of failures.

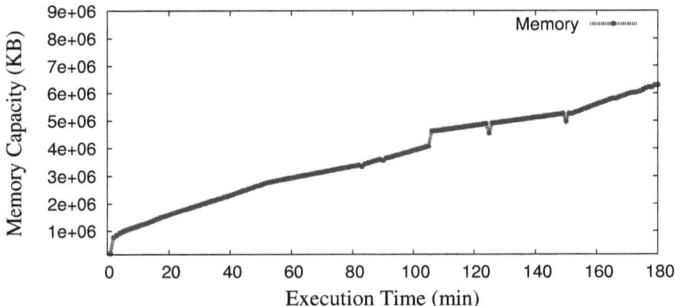

Figure 7.25: Monitored Memory Utilization

The monitored results of the memory usage are depicted in Figure 7.25. As shown in the figure, the memory consumption increases along the execution line of the TopHat workflow application. It is difficult to predict the total amount of memory the application might require in the next time interval or to successfully complete the data analysis. Thus, we define a threat threshold value that is about 2GB less than the current allocated memory. That is, once the memory utilization exceeds the threat threshold value, a notification message is sent to the knowledge database for resource allocation decisions.

Figure 7.26 shows the utilization of storage resource by the TopHat workflow application. According to the figure, the storage utilization increases along the execution line. In this case, one can notice some jumps in the utilization lines. These jumps can be high depending on the size of the data set to be analyzed. Therefore, the threat threshold value for managing storage resource is set to about 4GB less than the current allocated storage, in order not to risk failure situations before the knowledge management can react to allocate more storage resources.

Generally, the threat thresholds are defined to accommodate reaction time for the knowledge management so that the resource allocation procedures are carried out early enough before the system runs out of resources. In the next section, we discuss how the knowledge management deals with the notification messages.

Ensuring Resource Availability

This section shows via simulations how the knowledge management approach reacts to the monitored data and enables seamless workflow application execution, as well as an economically efficient use of resources. In order to demonstrate our approach, we simulate three scenarios,

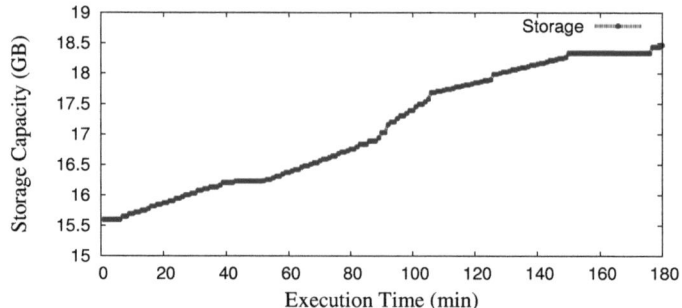

Figure 7.26: Monitored Storage Utilization

where we set up and manage our virtual machines (VMs) differently. In the first scenario, we assume a static configuration with a fixed initial resource configuration of the VMs. Normally, when setting up such a testbed as described in Section 7.6, an initial resource specification is done based on previously monitored data and earlier experiences.

The first ten measurements of CPU, memory, and storage lie in the range of [140, 12500] MIPS[3], [172, 1154] MB, [15.6,15.7] GB, respectively. So we initially configured our VMs with resource values greater than the maximum of the respective intervals, i.e., with 15000 MIPS of CPU, 4096 MB of memory, and 17.1 GB of storage. In the second scenario, we apply our knowledge management approach to these initial configurations. The third scenario presents a best case scenario, where we assume to have an oracle that predicts the maximal resource consumption that we statically set our VM configuration to. We use this scenario to compare the wastage in resource utilization.

The results presented in this section describe the number of resource violations, the achieved resource utilizations, as well as the number of reconfiguration actions, respectively, for every parameter in the different scenarios. These results are achieved by applying the scenarios to the monitored results of Figures 7.24, 7.25, and 7.26.

As shown in Figure 7.27, we experience violations in almost half of the cases for scenario 1. This is especially crucial for parameters *memory* and *storage*, where program execution would fail, if the system runs out of memory or storage, whereas for a violation of the *CPU* parameter, it would "only" degrade the performance and delay the successful termination of the workflow application. With scenario 2 we can reduce the SLA violations to a minimum. In this case, we completely avoid violations for *memory* and *storage*, and only encounter three violations for *CPU*. For scenario 3, we encounter no violations. However, this scenario wastes resources due to over-provisioning.

Figure 7.28 shows the resource utilization levels. It is clearly highest when a lot of violations

---

[3]The conversion of CPU utilization into MIPS is based on the assumption that an Intel Xeon(R) 3 GHz processor delivers 10000 MIPS for 100% resource utilization of one core, and linearly degrades with CPU utilization.

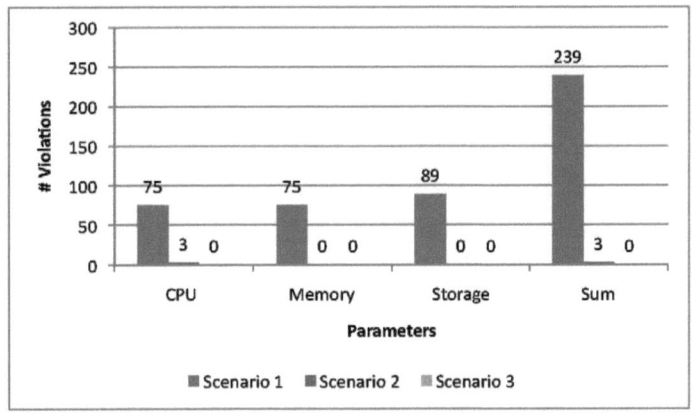

Figure 7.27: Number of Resource Violations in the Scenarios.

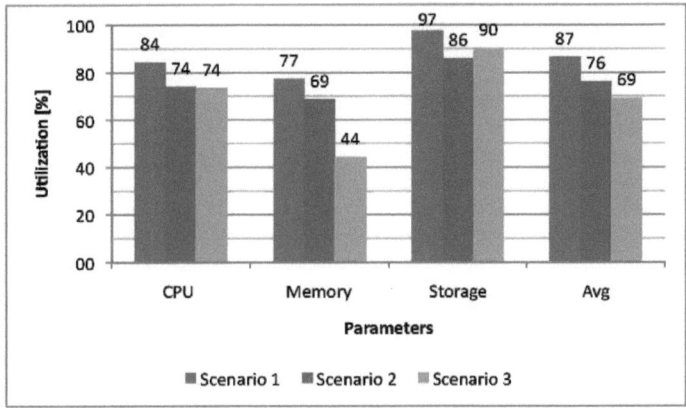

Figure 7.28: Resource Utilization Levels.

occur, so for Scenario 1. This holds because when a parameter is violated, then the resource is almost used up, meaning more of the resource would be needed to fulfill the needs. A huge advantage of Scenario 2 is that it does not run into any crucial SLA violation, but achieves a higher resource utilization (about 7% better on average) as compared to Scenario 3.

The numbers of autonomic resource reallocation actions are shown in Figure 7.29. Of

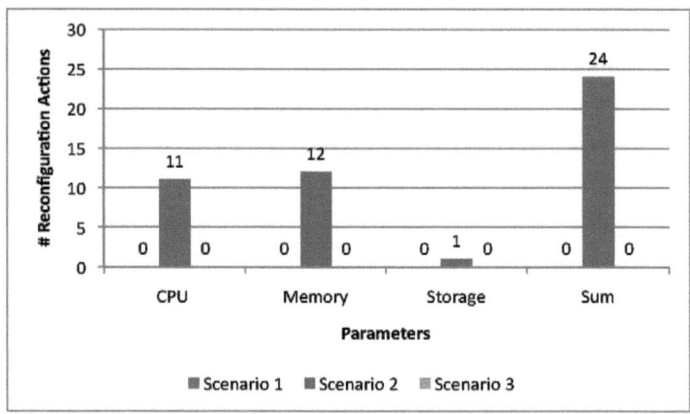

Figure 7.29: Reconfiguration Actions to Allocate Resources.

course, Scenarios 1 and 3 do not execute any reallocation action, but for the operations of the knowledge management in Scenario 2, the amount of executed reallocation actions stays very low, which means it does not affect the overall system performance.

According to our findings in [133], we set the threat thresholds $TT_{low} = 50\%$ and $TT_{high} = 75\%$ as discussed in Section 6.3.

Based on these observations, we conclude that by using the suggested Cloud management techniques we can guarantee the performance and successful completion of workflow applications. Furthermore, we can efficiently manage resources to avoid considerable wastage, extra maintenance costs, and CO_2 emissions due to the unnecessary energy consumption of unused resources.

The scientific workflow application used in this case study is simply an example. The realized autonomic Cloud management infrastructure is capable of supporting and managing the provisioning of different application types.

CHAPTER 8

Related Work

The related work presented in this thesis, shows the state of the art in Cloud management systems, especially on the monitoring, scheduling, and SLA management components. In this chapter, we divide and present the related work in four categories namely: i) Cloud infrastructure monitoring, ii) scheduling mechanism, iii) Cloud application monitoring, and iv) SLA enforcement and management. The following sections present their descriptions.

8.1 Cloud infrastructure Monitoring

In this section, we present the related work on infrastructure resource monitoring including mapping of low-level metrics to high-level SLA parameters. In analyzing the state-of-the-art literatures in this area, we also consider concepts in the related areas of Grid and Service-Oriented Architecture (SOA) based systems.

Fu *et al.* [78] propose GridEye, a service-oriented monitoring system with flexible architecture that is further equipped with an algorithm for prediction of the overall resource performance characteristics. The authors discuss how resources are monitored with their approach in Grid environment but they consider neither SLA management nor low-level metric mapping. Gunter *et al.* [86] present NetLogger, a distributed monitoring system, which can monitor and collect information of networks. Applications invoke NetLogger's API to survey the overload before and after some request or operation. However, it monitors only network resources. Wood *et al.* [186] developed a system, called Sandpiper, which automates the process of monitoring and detecting hotspots and remapping/reconfiguring VMs whenever necessary. Their monitoring system is reminiscent of our in terms of goal: avoid SLA violation. Similar to our approach, Sandpiper uses thresholds to check whether SLAs can be violated. However, it differs from our system by not considering the mapping of low level metrics, such as CPU and memory, to high-level SLA parameters, such as response time.

Katsaros *et al.* [98] present the architectural design and implementation of a service framework that monitors the resources of physical machines as well as virtual infrastructures. The proposed solution approaches the mentioned challenges through a service-oriented architectural

97

perspective, which offers the required level of flexibility and scalability to the monitoring infrastructure. But, their approach does not consider the mapping of low-level resource metrics. Baker *et al.* [10] propose GridRM - an open source generic resource monitoring architecture specifically designed for Grid. GridRM is designed to monitor resources rather than the applications that execute on a Grid. It is based on the Global Grid Forum monitoring architecture and it consists of components, such as SQL databases and SNMP agents. The architecture is implemented using Java technologies. However, their approach is focused only on Grid and does not consider resource monitoring in Clouds.

Mehrotra *et al.* [135] present an effective event based monitoring framework for distributed system hosted in virtualized environment. The authors aim to use the monitored information to control the distributed system in an autonomic manner to achieve or maintain the multidimensional QoS requirement of the deployed system while keeping minimal overhead and latency. Their approach uses Data Distribution Service (DDS) to realize publisher-subscriber communication model, which overcomes the traditional client-server model by offering extensive QoS configuration options. Nevertheless, their approach does not consider the definition of mapping rules and the mapping of low-level metrics to high-level SLA parameters. Viratanapanu *et al.* [178] discuss on-demand fine grained resource monitoring system for server consolidation. They describe the key information missing in the existing monitoring systems and present the design of Pantau - a monitoring system for capturing information necessary for server consolidation. However, they did not explain their resource monitoring strategy and how virtual machine resources are being mapped to monitor applications. Xiang *et al.* [189] propose VMDriver - a general and fine-grained approach for virtualization monitoring. In the design of their approach, the authors separated the event interception point in virtual machine monitor level and rich guest operating system reconstruction in the management domain. With this design, different monitoring drivers in the management domain can mask the differences of the guest operating systems in a large-scale distributed environment like Clouds. Their approach however, does not consider finding optimal measurement intervals for the monitoring of the virtual machine resources.

Huang *et al.* [95] discuss a combined push-pull model for resource monitoring in Cloud computing environments. Their approach is based on an extension of the prevailing push and pull model monitoring methods in Grids to Cloud computing. Their objective is to devise a monitoring framework capable to manage shared resources in Clouds. The motivation for this combination lies on the complementary characteristics of the two models. The push model has high consistency but low efficiency, whereas the pull model has low consistency but high efficiency. Thus, the authors combine these models by intelligently switching between them according to customer application requirements. Their approach however, does not deal with the determination of optimal measurement interval and the mapping of low-level resource metrics. Brandt *et al.* [26] propose resource monitoring and management with OVIS to enable HPC in Cloud computing environments. The aim of the authors is to enable high performance computing in Cloud environments through sophisticated resource allocation mechanisms. The authors argue that intelligent resource utilization is a key factor for enabling HPC applications. Resources are heterogeneous in Clouds, and are shared among users (particularly in virtualized environments) but there is a limited knowledge of the resource status. This leads to overheads and resource contention among VMs, which brings down the overall performance. In their approach, the authors address this issue by using an advanced monitoring tool to dynamically characterize the resource and application state, and use the resulting information to optimally assign and manage resources. Nevertheless, their approach does not consider monitoring of SLA objectives to ensure the performance of applications.

Andreolini *et al.* [8] present an assessment of overhead and scalability of system monitors for large data centers. The authors argue that there are several infrastructure monitoring tools designed to scale to very high numbers of physical machines, but such tools either collect performance measure at low frequency (missing to capture the dynamics of short-term task) or are not suitable for usage in Cloud environments. Therefore, with such tools monitoring the correctness and efficiency of live migration is very difficult. Thus, the authors focus on the assessment of the scalability limits of a realistic monitoring infrastructure and to identify the bottlenecks in monitoring large-scale Cloud environments. To this effect, they designed and tested a monitoring infrastructure prototype. However, their approach does not consider the scalability of mapping low-level resource metrics to high-level SLA parameter in Clouds. Voith *et al.* [179] propose a path supervision framework for service monitoring in Infrastructure as a Service (IaaS) platforms. Their approach considers network applications and the monitoring of their metrics. The proposed framework takes measurements during the application execution to monitor the performance and detect SLA violations. To achieve high scalability, the measurement strategy is structured into stages for monitoring specific parts of the infrastructure. The authors however, does not consider the monitoring of Cloud computational infrastructure resource metrics.

Rosenberg *et al.* [155] deal with QoS attributes for Web services. They identify important QoS attributes and their composition from resource metrics. They present mapping techniques for composing QoS attributes from resource metrics to form SLA parameters for a specific domain. However, they do not deal with monitoring of resource metrics. Bocciarelli *et al.* [52] introduce a model-driven approach for integrating performance prediction into service composition processes carried out by BPEL. In their approach, service SLA parameters are composed from system metrics using mapping techniques. Nevertheless, they consider neither resource metric monitoring nor SLA violation detection.

To address these open research challenges, we designed and implemented in this thesis, the Low-level Metrics to High-level SLA monitoring and mapping (LoM2HiS) framework, which monitors Cloud infrastructure resource metrics and maps the metric values to the equivalence of the high-level SLA parameter objectives in order to guarantee the performance of the user applications. Furthermore, we designed and implemented the Detecting SLA Violation Infrastructure (DeSVi) architecture, which is made up of components to setup virtual machines, deploy tasks, and monitor resources to detect service level objective violations. The architecture is also capable of determining optimal measurement interval for the monitoring operations.

8.2 Scheduling Mechanisms

The existing application scheduling strategies in Clouds are based on approaches developed in related areas such as distributed systems and Grids. Scheduling in these areas is mainly tailored towards ensuring single application SLA objectives. In the Cloud environments on the one hand, applications require guaranteeing numerous SLA objectives to achieve their QoS goals and on the other hand, resource utilization is of paramount importance to the Cloud provider.

Salehi et al. [156] propose market-oriented scheduling policies that consider resource prices and application deadlines. In their concept, they present two market-oriented scheduling algorithms. Their first algorithm known as time optimization policy aims at completing application execution as quickly as possible using available resources. The second algorithm known as cost optimization policy attempts to complete the application execution as economically as possible within the deadline. Their approach is limited to single task applications with single SLA objective and do not consider heterogenous applications requiring to ensure multiple SLA parameters. Pandey et al. [143] discuss a particle swarm optimization-based heuristic for scheduling workflow applications in Cloud computing environments. They focus on minimizing the total execution cost of applications on Cloud resources thereby achieving low computational cost and low data transmission cost. They do not consider resource utilization efficiency and moreover, their approach is targeted only at workflow applications. Garg et al. [80] present time and cost trade-off management for scheduling parallel applications on utility Grids. Their main goal is to manage the trade-off between time and cost such that applications can be executed most economically within a minimum time. They propose two scheduling heuristics for choosing the best Grid resources to achievie low cost while keeping to the application execution deadline. Their approach targets Grid applications in Grid-like environments.

Cao et al. [36] propose an optimized algorithm for task scheduling based on ABC (Activity Based Costing) in Clouds. They investigate the cost of scheduling different applications and the overhead the applications cause in resource allocation. Their approach considers cost as the only SLA objective for scheduling task in a Cloud environment. Lee et al. [116] discuss service request scheduling in Clouds based on achievable profits. They propose a pricing model using processor sharing for composite services in Clouds. In their work, two algorithms are devised whereby the first explicitly takes into account not only the profit achievable from the current service, but also the profit from other services being processed on the same service instance. The second algorithm attempts to minimize cost of renting resources from other infrastructure vendors. The approach of this work is similar to ours in the sense that it schedules service requests but it differs in the aspect that they only consider profit objectives for the provider and furthermore, they do not consider resource utilization, like in our case.

Wang et al. [180] present a load balancing algorithm for scheduling resources in Clouds according to task properties. The proposed scheduler combines OLB (Opportunistic Load Balancing) [102] and LBMM (Load Balance Min-Min) [187] scheduling algorithms that can efficiently utilize resources and maintain the load balancing of systems. The proposed scheduler aims to balance resource provisioning in a Cloud environment but does not consider the SLA objectives of the task being provisioned. Lu et al. [123] propose a load-adaptive Cloud resource scheduling model based on ant colony algorithm. Their approach uses real-time monitoring of virtual machine performance parameters and the ant colony algorithm strategies to schedule and balance workload among nodes in a Cloud environment. The goals of the authors are to meet changing load requirements and to improve efficiency of the resource utilization. However, their approach focuses on balancing the load among running nodes in Clouds and does not consider the SLA objectives of the executing applications in making decisions. Bo Yang et al. [192] discuss a utility-based job scheduling algorithm for Cloud computing considering reliability factors. The authors introduce failure and recovery scenarios in Cloud computing devices and propose a reenforcement based learning algorithm to make job scheduling fault tolerable while maximizing the utilities achieved in the long term. Their goals are to consider future system state and hardware/software failures in scheduling jobs, thus, they do not deal with guaranteeing of application performance objectives.

Yang *et al.* [193] present a cost-based resource scheduling paradigm in Clouds by leveraging market theory to schedule compute resources to fulfill customer requirements. It assigns a set of computing resources to customers according to resource availability and price. The authors describe a two-phase pattern for Cloud resource scheduling. In the first phase, resources are reserved for the virtual machines and in the second phase, the scheduling decisions are committed with those resources. They argue that these two phases must be atomic to avoid complexities and to increase performance. There approach, however, does not consider application scheduling and deployment. Hu *et al.* [94] propose a scheduling strategy on load balancing of virtual machine resources based on genetic algorithm in Cloud computing environments. The scheduling strategy computes ahead based on historical data and current state, the influence, deploying virtual machines would have on the system and chooses the least adverse effective solution. Through this means, it achieves load balancing and avoids dynamic migration cost. This strategy deals with the scheduling of virtual machines and does not consider the scheduling and deployment of applications. Zhong *et al.* [200] present an approach to optimized resource scheduling algorithm for open-source Cloud systems. In their approach, the authors investigate the possibility of allocating virtual machines in a flexible way to allow maximum usage of physical resources based on Improved Genetic Algorithm (IGA). With IGA, they use the idea of shortest genes and dividend policy in economics to select an optimal allocation for the virtual machines request. The most important step in the scheduling strategy is to find the fitness allocation using IGA where virtual machines would be deployed. This approach does not consider application scheduling and the guaranteeing of SLA objectives.

In this thesis, we addressed the application scheduling issues by designing and implementing a scheduling heuristic utilizing multiple SLA parameters in scheduling and deploying applications in Clouds. The scheduling heuristic is integrated with a load balancing mechanism to balance the application deployments among the running virtual machines. It also posses the ability to start new virtual machines for further deployments as long as the physical resources in the Cloud environment can accommodate them.

8.3 Application Monitoring in Clouds

The ability to monitor at application layer in Clouds provides the opportunity for efficient and cost-effective Cloud management. In this section, we analyze the exiting literatures in this area. In this analysis, we consider also Grid and service-oriented based systems, since they are related areas to Cloud computing.

Balis *et al.* [15] propose an infrastructure for Grid application monitoring. Their approach is based on OCM-G, which is a distributed monitoring system for obtaining information and manipulating applications running on the Grid. They aim to consider Grid-specific requirement and design a suitable monitoring architecture to be integrated into the OCM-G system. However, their approach considers only Grid specific applications. Bubak *et al.* [14] discuss the monitoring of Grid applications with Grid-Enabled OMIS monitor, which provides a standardized interface for accessing services. In their approach, they described the architecture of the system and provides some design details for the monitoring system to fit well in the Grid environment and support monitoring of interactive applications. Their monitoring goal is focused toward application development and they do not consider detecting application SLA violations. Kacsuk *et al.* [13] propose application monitoring in Grid with GRM and PROVE, which were originally developed as part of the P-GRADE graphical program development environment running on Clusters. In their work, they showed how they transformed GRM and PROVE into a standalone Grid monitoring tool. However, their approach does not consider automatic finding of optimal measurement intervals. Balaton *et al.* [12] discuss resource and job monitoring in the Grid. They presented a monitoring architecture with advanced functions like actuators and guaranteed data delivery. Their motivations toward application monitoring are to understand its internal operations and detect failure situations. They do not consider the monitoring of application resource consumption behaviours.

Rellermeyer *et al.* [150] propose the building, deploying, and monitoring of distributed applications with Eclipse. In their approach, they first analyse applications using Eclipse to determine the best way to deploy them in a distributed manner. After deploying the applications, they apply a tool to visualize the distributed execution of the applications and identify bottlenecks and failures. With this information they enforce the performance goals of the applications. However, they do not describe the usage of their approach in a large scale Cloud environment and moreover, their approach depends heavily on Eclipse framework. Kilpatrick *et al.* [101] present ChaosMon, an application for monitoring and displaying performance information for parallel and distributed systems. ChaosMon supports application developers in specifying performance metrics and to monitor these metrics visually to detect, analyze, and understand performance bottlenecks. This tool is a distributed monitor with a central control. It includes local monitors that reside on the target machines and communicate the monitored information to the central control. However, this tool has not been applied in Cloud environments and it does not support SLA violation detection. Wang *et al.* [181] discuss a scalable run-time correlation engine for monitoring in a Cloud computing environment. Their approach is based on the use of log files to determine the behaviour of distributed applications. Thus, they developed a framework for run-time correlation of distributed log files in a scalable manner for enterprise applications in a Cloud environment. The correlation engine is capable of analyzing and performing symptom matching with large volume of log data. But, it does not consider automatic determination of intervals for measuring/logging the application behaviours.

Clayman *et al.* [49] present Lattice framework for Cloud service monitoring in the RESERVOIR EU project. It is capable of monitoring physical resources, virtual machines and customized applications embedded with probes. Compared to our approach, the Lattice framework is not generic because its application monitoring capabilities are restricted to applications preconfigured with probes and it does not consider measurement intervals in its operation. Ferrer *et al.* [71] present the fundamentals for a toolkit for service platform architectures, which enable flexible and dynamic provisioning of Cloud services within the OPTIMIS EU project. The focus of the toolkit is aimed at optimizing the whole service lifecycle including service construction, deployment, and operation. It does neither detail the application monitoring strategy nor consider the determination of optimal measurement intervals. Xu *et al.* [45] propose an architecture for monitoring of multi-tenant systems whereby they aim to monitor QoS at tenant level to detect aggressive tenants consuming more resources as agreed. However, their architecture is theoretical. It is not yet implemented and there are no explanations of how to realize monitoring of resources consumed by a single tenant.

Shao *et al.* [161] present a performance guarantee for Cloud applications based on monitoring. The authors extract performance model from runtime monitored data using data mining techniques, which is then used to adjust the provisioning strategy to achieve a certain performance goals. They do not consider finding optimal measurement intervals in their approach. Rak *et al.* [149] propose Cloud application monitoring using the mOSAIC approach. In a first step, the authors describe the development of customized applications using mOSAIC API to be deployed on Cloud environments. For these applications, they propose in a second step some monitoring techniques. Their interest is only to gather information that can be used to perform manual or automatic load-balancing, increase/decrease the number of virtual machines or calculate the total cost of application execution. Their approach does not consider the detection of SLA violations to avoid SLA penalty cost and moreover, it is not generic since it monitors only applications developed using the mOSAIC API.

Jin *et al.* [162] discuss a performance guarantee approach based on a performance model, which is extracted from actual runtime monitoring data using data mining techniques. It considers two QoS metrics: *availability* and *response time*. To build the performance model, they analyze several attributes including number of CPU, number of application deployed on the same virtual machine, resource consumption, etc. However, their approach is not yet implemented and there are no evaluation results. Meng *et al.* [138] present REMO - a resource-aware application state monitoring for large-scale distributed system, which produces a forest of optimized monitoring trees through iterations of two procedures. The first procedure explores the chances of sharing per message processing overhead based on performance estimation while the second procedure refines the monitoring plan produced by the first procedure. The authors argue that careful planning of multiple application state monitoring task, by jointly considering multi-task optimization and resource-constrained monitoring tree construction, can facilitate much gain in scalability and performance. However, their approach do not consider automatic finding of optimal measurement interval for efficient application monitoring.

We addressed the open research challenges in application monitoring in this thesis, by proposing and implementing an application level monitoring architecture to monitor individually the resource consumption behaviours and the performance of each application executing on a shared host. In this approach, we also implemented an automatic mechanism for determining the optimal measurement intervals for the application monitoring. The ability to monitor at application level provides the opportunity of fine-grained management of Cloud application provisioning.

8.4 SLA Enforcement and Management

The management and enforcement of Service Level Agreement (SLA) in Clouds is not a trivial task. SLAs have become the basis for service provisioning in Cloud markets and therefore, an inevitable aspect of Cloud computing. In this section, we present existing concepts for the management of SLAs.

Boniface *et al.* [21] discuss dynamic service provisioning using GRIA (a Service Oriented Architecture framework) SLA. The authors explore how web service management using SLA and dynamic service provisioning can maximise resource utilization while fulfilling the QoS commitments to the existing customers. In their approach, they propose two possible policy enforcement strategies for handling SLA violation: i) prevention before violation and ii) reaction after violation. The prevention strategy is based on prediction of possible future violations, which can be obtained by monitoring predefined prevention thresholds. These prevention thresholds have to be defined on per SLA basis. With dynamic provisioning, when the prevention threshold is exceeded, a new service instance is started so that new requests are redirected to the new instance to ensure their SLA. The reaction strategy is only acceptable if the violation does not result in complete service failure. The service provider allows the violation of an SLA in order to enforce others. In such cases, it specifies priority for different SLAs based on business impact. Moreover, they do not detail how the low-level metric are monitored and mapped to high-level SLAs to enforce the application SLA objectives at runtime.

Koller *et al.* [106] discuss autonomous SLA management using a proxy-like approach. They implemented an architecture that can be exploited to define SLA contracts. The architecture allows autonomous management of such contracts, once service providers and customers explicitly provide the requirements for the contracts. Based on the architecture, they outlined some guidelines on how such a system can be setup and reused. Their strategy is based on WS-Agreement. Moreover, their approach is limited to Web services and does not consider other applications types. Frutos *et al.* [77] discuss the main approach of the EU project BREIN [27] to develop a framework that extends the characteristics of computational Grids by driving their usage inside new target areas in the business domain for advanced SLA management. BREIN applies SLA management to Grids, whereas we target SLA management in Clouds. Dobson *et al.* [56] present a unified QoS ontology applicable to QoS-based Web services selection, QoS monitoring, and QoS adaptation. However they do not consider the enforcement of other service application types. Comuzzi *et al.* [50] present an approach for establishment and monitoring of SLAs in complex service-based systems. They asserted that a service-provisioning infrastructure should allow the establishment of SLA contracts through coordinated negotiation among service providers and customers. In their approach, they define the process of SLA establishment adopted within the EU project SLA@SOI framework. They use WS-Agreement as the specification language and show the processes of negotiating electronic SLA between interested stakeholders. But they do not consider monitoring of low-level metrics and mapping them to high-level SLA parameters for ensuring the SLA objectives.

Ferretti *et al.* [73] propose QoS-aware Clouds. In their approach they discuss the design and evaluation of a middleware architecture that enables SLA-driven dynamic configurations to respond effectively to the QoS requirements of the Cloud customer applications. The proposed architecture is proactive. It uses continuous monitoring and dynamic resource allocation to enforce the agreed SLA objectives for the customer applications. However, they do not consider optimal monitoring interval for efficient monitoring and enforcement of SLA objectives. Skalkowski *et al.* [164] present the application of the ESB architecture for distributed monitoring of the SLA requirements. The authors identified some issues affecting efficient SLA enforcement processes such as different technologies for the evaluation of the SLA documents, complex deployment processes, and scalability issues. Their SLA enforcement strategy is based on the continuous monitoring of the system to identify violation situations. But they did not address the issues of individually enforcing customer SLAs for applications executing on the same host. Chen *et al.* [44] discuss Aspect Oriented Programming (AOP) based trustable SLA compliance monitoring for web services. The authors propose a novel trustable mechanism to monitor and evaluate SLA compliance based on the Aspect Oriented Programming paradigm. In their approach, authoritative monitoring features are supplied by a trustable SLA manager and by focusing the aspects into susceptible service runtime, provider can accurately monitor and report their service status. However, their approach targets only web services.

In our approach in this thesis, we addressed the issue of SLA management and enforcement through monitoring. We developed holistic monitoring techniques to monitor and detect SLA violation situations at different layers in Clouds. Furthermore, we developed mapping techniques and mapping rules to guide the mapping of the low-level resource metrics to the equivalence of high-level SLA parameters in order to enforce the agreed SLA objective. The correction of SLA violation situations in our approach, is realized with knowledge management techniques, which determine corrective actions based on the monitored information.

CHAPTER 9

Conclusion

This chapter presents the conclusion of the research work carried out in this thesis. We summary the contributions of this thesis and their implication to the advancement of autonomic resource and SLA management in Cloud computing. We present in Section 9.1 the summary of the thesis contributions and in Section 9.2, we discuss the issues not covered by our proposed solutions. Section 9.3 discusses the potential future work based on the limitations of the proposed solutions in this thesis.

9.1 Summary

In the course of this thesis, we have developed and implemented resource monitoring framework, application scheduling and deployment heuristic, and application monitoring architecture as basic components of a Cloud management infrastructure.

The contributed *LoM2HiS* framework provides infrastructure resource metrics monitoring and mapping features. It is capable of monitoring the low-level resource metrics and mapping them to the equivalence of the high-level SLA parameters using predefined mapping rules. The mapped SLA values together with predefined threat threshold forms the basis for monitoring application executions on virtual machines to guarantee their performance. The *LoM2HiS* framework has been applied in different areas of discipline including traffic management systems to monitor nodes in order to ensure their availability. Furthermore, we presented *DeSVi*—the novel architecture for monitoring and detecting SLA violations in Cloud computing infrastructures. It posses the capability of finding optimal measurement interval for application monitoring. The main components of the architecture are *the automatic VM deployer*, responsible for the allocation of resources and for mapping of tasks, *application deployer*, responsible for the execution of user applications, and the *LoM2HiS framework*, which monitors infrastructure resources and translates low-level metrics into high-level SLAs in order to monitors the execution of applications. Nevertheless, it features strategies for finding optimal measurement intervals for efficient resource and application monitoring. We evaluated the architecture using two use-case scenarios consisting of an image rendering application and a transactional application. From our experiments with these applications, we observed that there is no particular optimal suited measurement interval for all application types. It is easier to identify optimal intervals for applications with steady resource consumption, such as the 'vase' POV-Ray animation. However, applications with variable resource consumption require dynamic measurement intervals.

Scheduling and deployment strategies are means of achieving resource provisioning in Cloud environments. A further contribution of this thesis is the development of a novel scheduling heuristic considering multiple SLA objectives in deploying applications in Cloud environments. The heuristic includes load-balancing mechanism for efficient distribution of the applications' execution among the Cloud resources. We also presented a flexible on-demand resource usage feature included in the heuristic for automatically starting new VMs when non-appropriate VM is available for the application deployments. We discussed in details the design of the heuristic and its implementations. We evaluated the proposed scheduling heuristic using the CloudSim simulation tool.

In order to manage the deployment of multiple applications on a single virtual machine, we proposed an application monitoring architecture (CASViD), which monitors and detects SLA violations at the application layer in Cloud environments. We evaluated the architecture on a real Cloud testbed using three types of image rendering application workloads with heterogeneous behaviours necessary to investigate different application provisioning scenarios and to automatically determine the optimal measurement intervals to monitor the application provisioning. From our experiments, the proposed architecture is efficient in monitoring and detecting individual application SLA violation situations. Furthermore, we observed that one can automatically find the optimal measurement intervals by sampling different ones and checking their net utility values. With the realization of CASViD, we achieved the capabilities of monitoring and detecting SLA violations of single customer applications being provisioned in a shared host. And thus, in addition to our previous resource monitoring techniques, we realized a holistic monitoring model capable of monitoring at different layers in Clouds.

Apart from our investigations on monitoring strategies and SLA violation detection, we integrated knowledge management techniques into the Cloud management infrastructure to achieve autonomic behaviour and to propose reactive actions to prevent or correct the SLA violation situations. Monitoring capabilities facilitate best reactive actions, which leads to the realization of our goal of achieving an autonomic Cloud management infrastructure.

9.2 Constraints on Thesis Contributions

In this section, we describe the limitations of the research contributions achieved within this thesis as stated in Section 1.3. These issues are important for proper understanding of the proposed solutions and they highlight things that are out of scope in our considerations. The following points describe the constraints on the proposed solutions.

- The proposed LoM2HiS framework includes small number of mapping rules. At the current state, it covers only few applications such as POV-Ray, Online Web shop application, and scientific workflows. It is not fully generic and does not posses mapping rules for other application types. In the design of the LoM2HiS framework, we used relational database such as MySQL. We did not try NoSQL databases such as Hadoop. Furthermore, we did not investigate on models to automatically generate the threat thresholds used in the detection of future SLA violation threats. We manually derived the threat threshold values based on the predefined SLA objectives.

- The DeSVi architecture is currently capable of monitoring only single Cloud data centers. It is not capable of monitoring federated Cloud environment where multiple Cloud data centers are involved. The SLA objectives used to guide the performance of the application are defined based on some sample runs. This method alone might not be sufficient for defining SLA objectives for dynamical applications. Other methods should be investigated.

- The proposed scheduling heuristic integrated with load balancing mechanism considers only computational resource SLA objectives in scheduling and deploying applications. It does not directly consider non-functional SLA parameters like *response time* in its operation. It implicitly assumes fulfilling the resource requirements of applications implies the guaranteeing of their performance. This scheduling heuristic does not consider energy efficiency objectives in scheduling and deploying applications in Clouds. This aspect is very essential as providers are now seeking for ways of reducing the energy consumption of their Cloud environments.

- The application monitoring architecture (CASViD) is only tested in a Cloud environment with about 36 virtual machines. We assume that it could be applied in a large scale Cloud environment based on its design concept. However, it has not been tested in a large scale Cloud environment. Furthermore, in our evaluations, we monitored only computational intensive applications. The architecture has not been applied to monitor transactional applications.

9.3 Future Work

As discussed in Section 9.2, it can be observed that some important issues are out of scope regarding our proposed monitoring and scheduling solutions in this thesis. These issues imply open research challenges in this area. Further research efforts might consider the following:

- The mapping of the low-level metrics to the equivalence of the high-level SLA parameters proves to be a useful strategy for guaranteeing the performance of applications in Clouds. However, the definition of the mapping rules is not straight forward. To support the broad usage of this strategy, there are need to develop database of mapping rules covering different types of applications. In this process, one could create groups of applications using the same mapping rules in order to avoid complexities. Another interesting issue to be investigated is the generation of threat thresholds for the prediction of future SLA violations. Automatic models should be designed to address this issue.

- Cloud computing promises high scalability and the support of large number of users accessing services concurrently. The use of relational database in Clouds has been problematic in terms of scalability and performance [88]. Potential solutions to this challenge is the use of NoSQL databases [87]. Extending the LoM2HiS framework with NoSQL database will help improve its scalability and its usage in large scale Cloud environment. Furthermore, it will help create basis for interoperation with commercial Cloud providers such as Amazon EC2.

- To fully utilize the features of Cloud computing and to further reduce cost, there are needs for collaboration among Cloud providers in the form of federation [84]. The Cloud federation mechanism avoids the problem of owning a limited amount of resources by Cloud providers, which empowers a provider to outsource resources to other providers in case of variation in demand. The management of Cloud federations requires appropriate monitoring techniques and communication channels [40]. Thus, it is necessary to extend the proposed monitoring techniques to address these challenges.

- The proposed scheduling heuristic can be further improved by integrating monitoring techniques into its operations. Through this means, the scheduler will acquire the current resource status and will have the capability of making decisions at runtime. Furthermore, monitoring technique will provide the scheduler with information about the non-functional performance objectives of the executing applications in order to make better future decisions. Another aspect of scheduling to be investigated is on energy efficiency, where models and strategies for conserving energy in a Cloud environment will be studied. Nevertheless, the scheduling and deployment of applications in federated Cloud environment considering different outsourcing strategies are still open research challenges.

- Based on the developed monitoring techniques in this thesis, one can investigate security issues in Cloud environment. That is, one can use the monitoring techniques to monitor security relevant components in Clouds. This can lead to the study of security models and strategies in Clouds.

We anticipate that further research work on Cloud monitoring and application scheduling will in general be related to these open research challenges.

Bibliography

[1] Agnar Aamodt and Enric Plaza. Case-based reasoning: Foundational issues, methodological variations, and system approaches. *AI Communications*, 7:39–59, 1994.

[2] David Abramson, Rajkumar Buyya, and Jonathan Giddy. A computational economy for grid computing and its implementation in the nimrod-g resource broker. *Future Generation Computer System*, 18(8):1061–1074, October 2002.

[3] ActiveMQ. Messaging and integration pattern provider. http://activemq.apache.org/ (Last Access: April 3, 2012).

[4] Lars Albertsson. Holistic debugging – enabling instruction set simulation for software quality assurance. In *14th IEEE International Symposium on Modeling, Analysis, and Simulation of Computer and Telecommunication Systems, 2006. MASCOTS 2006.*, pages 96 – 103, September 2006.

[5] Ilkay Altintas, Chad Berkley, Efrat Jaeger, Matthew Jones, Bertram Ludascher, and Steve Mock. Kepler: an extensible system for design and execution of scientific workflows. *Scientific and Statistical Database Management, 16th International Conference on*, pages 423 – 424, 2004.

[6] Amazon. Amazon elastic computing cloud. http://aws.amazon.com/ec2/ (Last Access: April 3, 2012).

[7] Rachid Anane. Autonomic behaviour in qos management. In *Third International Conference on Autonomic and Autonomous Systems, 2007. ICAS07.*, page 57, June 2007.

[8] Mauro Andreolini, Michele Colajanni, and Riccardo Lancellotti. Assessing the overhead and scalability of system monitors for large data centers. In *Proceedings of the First International Workshop on Cloud Computing Platforms*, CloudCP '11, pages 3:1–3:7, 2011.

[9] J. Appavoo, Kai Hui, C. A. N. Soules, R. W. Wisniewski, D. M. Da Silva, O. Krieger, M. A. Auslander, D. J. Edelsohn, B. Gamsa, G. R. Ganger, P. McKenney, Michael Ostrowski, B. Rosenburg, Michael Stumm, and Jimi Xenidis. Enabling autonomic behavior in systems software with hot swapping. *IBM Systems Journal*, 42(1):60 –76, 2003.

[10] Mark Baker and Garry Smith. Gridrm: A resource monitoring architecture for the grid. In *Proceedings of the Third International Workshop on Grid Computing*, GRID '02, pages 268–273, 2002.

[11] Ponnuram Balakrishnan and Thamarai Selvi Somasundaram. SLA enabled CARE resource broker. *Future Generation Computer Systems*, 27(3):265 – 279, 2011.

[12] Zoltán Balaton and Gábor Gombás. Resource and job monitoring in the grid. In *Proceedings of the International Conference on Parallel and Distributed Computing (Euro-Par'03)*, pages 404–411, 2003.

[13] Zoltán Balaton, Péter Kacsuk, and Norbert Podhorszki. Application monitoring in the grid with grm and prove. In *Proceedings of the International Conference on Computational Sciences-Part I*, ICCS '01, pages 253–262, 2001.

[14] Bartosz Balis, Marian Bubak, Wlodzimierz Funika, Tomasz Szepieniec, Roland Wismueller, and Marcin Radecki. Monitoring grid applications with grid-enabled omis monitor. In *Grid Computing*, volume 2970, pages 230–239, 2004.

[15] Bartosz Balis, Marian Bubak, Wodzimierz Funika, Tomasz Szepieniec, and Roland Wismüller. An infrastructure for grid application monitoring. In *Proceedings of the 9th European PVM/MPI Users' Group Meeting on Recent Advances in Parallel Virtual Machine and Message Passing Interface*, pages 41–49, 2002.

[16] Caroline Barelle, E. Vellidou, and D. Koutsouris. The biotelekinesy home care service: A holistic concept to prevent fall among the elderly based on ict and computer vision. In *2010 10th IEEE International Conference on Information Technology and Applications in Biomedicine (ITAB)*, pages 1 – 5, November 2010.

[17] Paul Barham, Boris Dragovic, Keir Fraser, Steven Hand, Tim Harris, Alex Ho, Rolf Neugebauer, Ian Pratt, and Andrew Warfield. Xen and the art of virtualization. In *Proceedings of the nineteenth ACM symposium on Operating systems principles*, SOSP '03, pages 164–177, 2003.

[18] Anton Beloglazov and Rajkumar Buyya. Energy efficient resource management in virtualized cloud data centers. In *Proceedings of the 2010 10th IEEE/ACM International Conference on Cluster, Cloud and Grid Computing*, CCGRID '10, pages 826–831, Washington, DC, USA, 2010. IEEE Computer Society.

[19] Josep Ll. Berral, Íñigo Goiri, Ramón Nou, Ferran Julià, Jordi Guitart, Ricard Gavaldà, and Jordi Torres. Towards energy-aware scheduling in data centers using machine learning. In *Proceedings of the 1st International Conference on Energy-Efficient Computing and Networking*, e-Energy '10, pages 215–224, 2010.

[20] Irena Bojanova and Augustine Samba. Analysis of cloud computing delivery architecture models. In *2011 IEEE Workshops of International Conference on Advanced Information Networking and Applications (WAINA)*, pages 453 –458, March 2011.

[21] Mike Boniface, Stephen C. Phillips, and Alfonso Sanchez-macian. Dynamic service provisioning using GRIA SLAs. In *Proceedings of the 5th International Workshops on Service-Oriented Computing (ICSOC'07)*, 2007.

[22] Jacques Bouman, Jos Trienekens, and Mark Van der Zwan. Specification of service level agreements, clarifying concepts on the basis of practical research. In *STEP '99. Proceedings of Software Technology and Engineering Practice, 1999*, pages 169–178, 1999.

[23] Ivona Brandic. Towards self-manageable cloud services. In *33rd Annual IEEE International Computer Software and Applications Conference, 2009. COMPSAC '09.*, volume 2, pages 128–133, July 2009.

[24] Ivona Brandic, Dejan Music, and Schahram Dustdar. Vieslaf framework: Facilitating negotiations in clouds by applying service mediation and negotiation bootstrapping. *Scalable Computing: Practice and Experiences (SCPE), Special Issue of Scalabe Computing on Grid Applications and Middleware & Large Scale Computations in Grids*, 11(2):189–204, June 2010.

[25] Ivona Brandic, Dejan Music, Schahram Dustdar, Srikumar Venugopal, and Rajkumar Buyya. Advanced qos methods for grid workflows based on meta-negotiations and sla-mappings. In *Third Workshop on Workflows in Support of Large-Scale Science, 2008. WORKS 2008.*, pages 1–10, November 2008.

[26] Jim Brandt, Ann Gentile, Jackson Mayo, Philippe P ébay, Diana Roe, David Thompson, and Matthew Wong. Resource monitoring and management with ovis to enable hpc in cloud computing environments. In *IPDPS 2009. IEEE International Symposium on Parallel Distributed Processing 2009.*, pages 1–8, May 2009.

[27] Brein. Business objective driven reliable and intelligent grids for real business. http://www.eu-brein.com/ (Last Access: April 3, 2012).

[28] Ivan Breskovic, Christian Haas, Simon Caton, and Ivona Brandic. Towards self-awareness in cloud markets: A monitoring methodology. In *9th IEEE International Conference on Dependable, Autonomic and Secure Computing (DASC 2011)*, pages 81–88, December 2011.

[29] Ivan Breskovic, Michael Maurer, Vincent C. Emeakaroha, Ivona Brandic, and Joern Altmann. Towards autonomic market management in cloud computing infrastructures. In *International Conference on Cloud Computing and Services Science (CLOSER 2011)*, May 2011.

[30] Ivan Breskovic, Michael Maurer, Vincent C. Emeakaroha, Ivona Brandic, and Schahram Dustdar. Cost-efficient utilization of public sla templates in autonomic cloud markets. In *4th IEEE International Conference on Utility and Cloud Computing (UCC 2011)*, pages 229–236, December 2011.

[31] Rajkumar Buyya, Chee Shin Yeo, Srikumar Venugopal, James Broberg, and Ivona Brandic. Cloud computing and emerging IT platforms: Vision, hype, and reality for delivering computing as the 5th utility. *Future Generation Computer Systems*, 25(6):599–616, 2009.

[32] Rodrigo N. Calheiros, Rajkumar Buyya, and Cesar A. F. De Rose. A heuristic for mapping virtual machines and links in emulation testbeds. In *International Conference on Parallel Processing, 2009. ICPP '09.*, pages 518 –525, September 2009.

[33] Rodrigo N. Calheiros, Rajkumar Buyya, and Cesar. A. F. De Rose. Building an automated and self-configurable emulation testbed for grid applications. *Software: Practice and Experience*, 40(5):405–429, 2010.

[34] Rodrigo N. Calheiros, Rajiv Ranjan, Anton Beloglazov, Cesar A. F. De Rose, and Rajkumar Buyya. Cloudsim: a toolkit for modeling and simulation of cloud computing environments and evaluation of resource provisioning algorithms. *Software: Practice and Experience*, 41:23–50, January 2011.

[35] Cinzia Cantacessi, Aaron R. Jex, Ross S. Hall, Neil D. Young, Bronwyn E. Campbell, Anja Joachim, Matthew J. Nolan, Sahar Abubucker, Paul W. Sternberg, Shoba Ranganathan, Makedonka Mitreva, and Robin B. Gasser. A practical, bioinformatic workflow system for large data sets generated by next-generation sequencing. *Nucleic Acids Research*, 38(17):e171, 2010.

[36] Qi Cao, Zhi-Bo Wei, and Wen-Mao Gong. An optimized algorithm for task scheduling based on activity based costing in cloud computing. In *3rd International Conference on Bioinformatics and Biomedical Engineering ICBBE 2009.*, pages 1 –3, June. 2009.

[37] Henri Casanova, Graziano Obertelli, Francine Berman, and Richard Wolski. The apples parameter sweep template: User-level middleware for the grid. *Scientific Programming*, 8(3):111–126, August 2000.

[38] Jeffrey D. Case, M. Fedor, Martin L. Schoffstall, and J. Davin. Simple network management protocol (snmp), 1990.

[39] Antonio Celesti, Francesco Tusa, Massimo Villari, and Antonio Puliafito. How to enhance cloud architectures to enable cross-federation. In *Proceedings of the 2010 IEEE 3rd International Conference on Cloud Computing*, CLOUD '10, pages 337–345, 2010.

[40] Antonio Celesti, Francesco Tusa, Massimo Villari, and Antonio Puliafito. How to enhance cloud architectures to enable cross-federation. In *2010 IEEE 3rd International Conference on Cloud Computing (CLOUD)*, pages 337 –345, July 2010.

[41] Antonio Celesti, Francesco Tusa, Massimo Villari, and Antonio Puliafito. Three-phase cross-cloud federation model: The cloud sso authentication. In *Proceedings of the 2010 Second International Conference on Advances in Future Internet*, AFIN '10, pages 94–101, 2010.

[42] Rajiv Chakravorty, Jon Crowcroft, Ian Pratt, and Maurizio D'Arienzo. Dynamic sla-based qos control for third generation wireless networks: the cadenus extension. In *IEEE International Conference on Communications, 2003. ICC '03.*, volume 2, pages 938 – 943, May 2003.

[43] Clovis Chapman, Wolfgang Emmerich, Fermín Galán Márquez, Stuart Clayman, and Alex Galis. Elastic service definition in computational clouds. In *2010 IEEE/IFIP Network Operations and Management Symposium Workshops (NOMS Wksps)*, pages 327 –334, April 2010.

[44] Congwu Chen, Lei Li, and Jun Wei. Aop based trustable sla compliance monitoring for web services. In *Seventh International Conference on Quality Software, 2007. QSIC '07.*, pages 225 –230, oct. 2007.

[45] Xu Cheng, Yuliang Shi, and Qingzhong Li. A multi-tenant oriented performance monitoring, detecting and scheduling architecture based on sla. In *2009 Joint Conferences on Pervasive Computing (JCPC)*, pages 599 – 604, December 2009.

[46] Yu Cheng and Weihua Zhuang. Dynamic inter-sla resource sharing in path-oriented differentiated services networks. *IEEE/ACM Transactions on Networking*, 14(3):657 –670, June 2006.

[47] Inderpreet Chopra and Maninder Singh. Analysing the need for autonomic behaviour in grid computing. In *2010 The 2nd International Conference on Computer and Automation Engineering (ICCAE),*, volume 1, pages 535 –539, February 2010.

[48] Wu-Chun Chung and Ruay-Shiung Chang. A new mechanism for resource monitoring in grid computing. *Future Generation Computer Systems*, 25(1):1–7, 2009.

[49] Stuart CLAYMAN, Alex GALIS, Clovis CHAPMAN, Giovanni TOFFETTI, Luis RODERO-MERINO, Luis M. VAQUERO, Kenneth NAGIN, and Benny ROCHWERGER. Monitoring future internet service clouds. In *Towards the Future Internet - A European Research Perspective book*, April 2010.

[50] Marco Comuzzi, Constantinos Kotsokalis, George Spanoudakis, and Ramin Yahyapour. Establishing and monitoring slas in complex service based systems. In *Proceedings of the 2009 IEEE 7th International Conference on Web Services*, ICWS '09, pages 783–790, 2009.

[51] Anacleto Correia and Fernando Brito e Abreu. Defining and observing the compliance of service level agreements: A model driven approach. In *2010 Seventh International Conference on the Quality of Information and Communications Technology (QUATIC)*, pages 165 –170, October 2010.

[52] Andrea D'Ambrogio and Paolo Bocciarelli. A model-driven approach to describe and predict the performance of composite services. In *Proceedings of the 6th international workshop on Software and performance*, WOSP '07, pages 78–89, 2007.

[53] A. Dan, D. Davis, R. Kearney, A. Keller, R. King, D. Kuebler, H. Ludwig, M. Polan, M. Spreitzer, and A. Youssef. Web services on demand: Wsla-driven automated management. *IBM Systems Journal*, 43(1):136 –158, 2004.

[54] Tom De Wolf, Giovanni Samaey, and Dirk Roose. Decentralised autonomic computing: Analysing self-organising emergent behaviour using advanced numerical methods. In *Proceedings. Second International Conference on Autonomic Computing, 2005. ICAC 2005*, pages 52 –63, June 2005.

[55] Ewa Deelman, Gurmeet Singh, Mei-Hui Su, James Blythe, Yolanda Gil, Carl Kesselman, Gaurang Mehta, Karan Vahi, G. Bruce Berriman, John Good, Anastasia Laity, Joseph C. Jacob, and Daniel S. Katz. Pegasus: A framework for mapping complex scientific workflows onto distributed systems. *Sci. Program.*, 13:219–237, July 2005.

[56] Glen Dobson and Alfonso Sanchez-Macian. Towards unified QoS/SLA ontologies. In *IEEE Services Computing Workshops, 2006. SCW '06.*, pages 169 –174, September 2006.

[57] Sandrine Duflos, Valerie Gay, Brigitte Kervella, and Eric Horlait. Integration of security parameters in the service level specification to improve qos management of secure distributed multimedia services. In *19th International Conference on Advanced Information Networking and Applications, 2005. AINA 2005.*, volume 2, pages 145 – 148, March 2005.

[58] Erik Elmroth and Johan Tordsson. A grid resource broker supporting advance reservations and benchmark-based resource selection. In *Proceedings of the 7th international conference on Applied Parallel Computing: state of the Art in Scientific Computing*, PARA'04, pages 1061–1070, 2006.

[59] Vincent C. Emeakaroha, Ivona Brandic, Michael Maurer, and Ivan Breskovic. Sla-aware application deployment and resource allocation in clouds. In *2011 IEEE 35th Annual Computer Software and Applications Conference Workshops (COMPSACW)*, pages 298 –303, July 2011.

[60] Vincent C. Emeakaroha, Ivona Brandic, Michael Maurer, and Schahram Dustdar. Low level metrics to high level slas - lom2his framework: Bridging the gap between monitored metrics and sla parameters in cloud environments. In *2010 International Conference on High Performance Computing and Simulation (HPCS)*, pages 48 –54, July 2010.

[61] Vincent C. Emeakaroha, Ivona Brandic, Michael Maurer, and Schahram Dustdar. Cloud resource provisioning and sla enforcement via lom2his framework. *Concurrency and Computation: Practice and Experience*, 2011.

[62] Vincent C. Emeakaroha, Rodrigo N. Calheiros, Marco A. S. Netto, Ivona Brandic, and César A. F. De Rose. DeSVi: An architecture for detecting SLA violations in cloud computing infrastructures. In *Proceedings of the 2nd International ICST Conference on Cloud Computing (CloudComp'10)*, 2010.

[63] Vincent C. Emeakaroha, Tiago C. Ferreto, Marco A. S. Netto, Ivona Brandic, and Cesar A. F. De Rose. Casvid: Application level monitoring for sla violation detection in clouds. In *36th Annual IEEE Computer and Application International Conference (COMPSAC 2012)*, July 2012.

[64] Vincent C. Emeakaroha, Pawel P. Labaj, Michael Maurer, Ivona Brandic, and David P. Kreil. Optimizing bioinformatics workflows for data analysis using cloud management techniques. In *Proceedings of the 6th workshop on Workflows in support of large-scale science*, WORKS '11, pages 37–46. ACM, 2011.

[65] Vincent C. Emeakaroha, Michael Maurer, Ivona Brandic, and Schahram Dustdar. Fosii - foundations of self-governing ict infrastructures. *Special Theme: Cloud Computing Platforms, Software, and Applications. ERCIM News*, 83:40–41, October 2010.

[66] Vincent C. Emeakaroha, Michael Maurer, Ivan Breskovic, Ivona Brandic, and Schahram Dustdar. Soa and qos management for cloud computing. In Lizhe Wang, Rajiv Ranjan, Jinjun Chen, and Boualem Benatallah, editors, *Cloud Computing: Methodology, System, and Applications*. CRC, Taylor & Francis Group, 2011.

[67] Vincent C. Emeakaroha, Marco A. S. Netto, Rodrigo N. Calheiros, and Cesar A. F. De Rose. Achieving flexible sla and resource management in clouds. In Massimo Villari, Ivona Brandic, and Francesco Tusa, editors, *Achieving Federated and Self-Manageable Cloud Infrastructures: Theory and Practice*. IGI Global, 2012.

[68] Vincent C. Emeakaroha, Marco A.S. Netto, Rodrigo N. Calheiros, Ivona Brandic, Rajkumar Buyya, and Cesar A.F. De Rose. Towards autonomic detection of sla violations in cloud infrastructures. *Future Generation Computer Systems*, 2011.

[69] ESPER. Event stream processing. http://esper.codehaus.org/ (Last Access: April 3, 2012).

[70] Wang Fei and Li Fan-Zhang. The design of an autonomic computing model and the algorithm for decision-making. In *2005 IEEE International Conference on Granular Computing,*, volume 1, pages 270–273, July 2005.

[71] Ana J. Ferrer. Optimis: a holistic approach to cloud service provisioning. http://www.optimis-project.eu/ (Last Access: April 4, 2012).

[72] Tiago C. Ferreto, Cesar A. F. De Rose, and Luiz De Rose. Rvision: An open and high configurable tool for cluster monitoring. In *CCGRID'02*, 2002.

[73] Stefano Ferretti, Vittorio Ghini, Fabio Panzieri, Michele Pellegrini, and Elisa Turrini. Qos-aware clouds. In *2010 IEEE 3rd International Conference on Cloud Computing*, pages 321–328, 2010.

[74] FoSII. Foundations of self-governing infrastructures. http://www.infosys.tuwien.ac.at/linksites/FOSII/index.html (Last Access: April 3, 2012).

[75] Ian Foster, Carl Kesselman, and Steven Tuecke. The anatomy of the grid: Enabling scalable virtual organizations. *International Journal of High Performance Computing Applicaltions*, 15:200–222, August 2001.

[76] FreeCBR. FreeCBR. http://freecbr.sourceforge.net/ (Last Access: April 4, 2012).

[77] Henar M. Frutos and Ioannis Kotsiopoulos. BREIN: Business objective driven reliable and intelligent grids for real business. *International Journal of Interoperability in Business Information Systems*, 3(1):39–42, 2009.

[78] Wei Fu and Qian Huang. Grideye: A service-oriented grid monitoring system with improved forecasting algorithm. In *Proceedings of the Fifth International Conference on Grid and Cooperative Computing Workshops*, GCCW '06, pages 5–12, 2006.

[79] Bundesanstalt für Strassenwesen (BaSt). Technische Lieferbedingungen für Streckenstationen, 2002.

[80] Saurabh Kumar Garg, Rajkumar Buyya, and Howard Jay Siegel. Time and cost tradeoff management for scheduling parallel applications on utility grids. *Future Generation Computing System*, 26(8):1344–1355, 2010.

[81] Nathan H. Gartner, C. Stamatiadis, and Philip J. Tarnoff. Development of real time, traffic-adaptive control strategies for IVHS. In *Proceedings of the First World Congress on Applications of Transport Telematics and Intelligent Vehicle-Highway Systems*, volume 2, pages 423–430, 1994.

[82] Jessica Gerchak, Mary Besterfield-Sacre, Lary J. Shuman, and Harvey Wolje. Using concept maps for evaluating program objectives. In *FIE 2003 33rd Annual Frontiers in Education, 2003.*, volume 1, pages T3B – 20–5 Vol.1, November 2003.

[83] Jeremy Goecks, Anton Nekrutenko, James Taylor, and The Galaxy Team. Galaxy: a comprehensive approach for supporting accessible, reproducible, and transparent computational research in the life sciences. *Genome Biology*, 11(8):R86, 2010.

[84] Inigo Goiri, Jordi Guitart, and Jordi Torres. Characterizing cloud federation for enhancing providers' profit. In *2010 IEEE 3rd International Conference on Cloud Computing (CLOUD)*, pages 123 –130, July 2010.

[85] Google. Google appengine. https://developers.google.com/appengine/ (Last Access: April 3, 2012).

[86] Dan Gunter, Brian Tierney, Brian Crowley, Mason Holding, and Jason Lee. Netlogger: A toolkit for distributed system performance analysis. In *Proceedings of the 8th International Symposium on Modeling, Analysis and Simulation of Computer and Telecommunication Systems*, MASCOTS '00, pages 267– 273, 2000.

[87] Jing Han, E. Haihong, Guan Le, and Jian Du. Survey on nosql database. In *2011 6th International Conference on Pervasive Computing and Applications (ICPCA)*, pages 363 –366, October 2011.

[88] Jing Han, Meina Song, and Junde Song. A novel solution of distributed memory nosql database for cloud computing. In *2011 IEEE/ACIS 10th International Conference on Computer and Information Science (ICIS)*, pages 351 –355, may 2011.

[89] Shenin Hassan, Dhiya Al-Jumeily, and Abir Jaafar Hussain. Autonomic computing paradigm to support system's development. In *2009 Second International Conference on Developments in eSystems Engineering (DESE)*, pages 273 –278, December 2009.

[90] Peer Hasselmeyer and Nico d'Heureuse. Towards holistic multi-tenant monitoring for virtual data centers. In *Network Operations and Management Symposium Workshops*, pages 350 –356, 2010.

[91] Hibernate. Relational persistence for java and .net. http://www.hibernate.org/ (Last Access: April 3, 2012).

[92] Micha Hofri. A probablistic analysis of the next-fit bin packing algorithm. *Journal of Algorithms*, 5:547–556, 1984.

[93] David Hollingsworth. The workflow reference model. In *Technical Report (WFMC-TC00-1003) Workflow Management Coalition*, 1995.

[94] Jinhua Hu, Jianhua Gu, Guofei Sun, and Tianhai Zhao. A scheduling strategy on load balancing of virtual machine resources in cloud computing environment. In *2010 Third International Symposium on Parallel Architectures, Algorithms and Programming (PAAP)*, pages 89 –96, December 2010.

[95] He Huang and Liqiang Wang. P & P: A combined push-pull model for resource monitoring in cloud computing environment. In *2010 IEEE 3rd International Conference on Cloud Computing (CLOUD)*, pages 260 – 267, July 2010.

[96] Duncan Hull, Katy Wolstencroft, Robert Stevens, Carole Goble, Mathew R. Pocock, Peter Li, and Tom Oinn. Taverna: a tool for building and running workflows of services. *Nucleic Acids Research*, 34(suppl 2):W729–W732, 1 July 2006.

[97] JMS. Java messaging service. http://java.dzone.com/articles/all-about-jms-messages (Last Access: April 4, 2012).

[98] Gregory Katsaros, Roland Kubert, and Georgina Gallizo. Building a service-oriented monitoring framework with rest and nagios. In *2011 IEEE International Conference on Services Computing (SCC)*, pages 426 –431, July 2011.

[99] Jeffrey O. Kephart and David. M. Chess. The vision of autonomic computing. *IEEE Computer*, 36(1):41–50, 2003.

[100] Mandeep Khella, Tony Martin, John T. Pearson, and Roger Dixon. Systems approach for health management design: A simple fuel system case study. In *2010 5th International Conference on System of Systems Engineering (SoSE)*, pages 1 – 6, June 2010.

[101] Carol Kilpatrick and Karsten Schwan. Chaosmon - application-specific monitoring and display of performance information for parallel and distributed systems. In *Proceedings of the 1991 ACM/ONR workshop on Parallel and distributed debugging*, PADD '91, pages 57–67, 1991.

[102] Tae W. Kim, Tae-Young Min, and Chung G. Kang. Opportunistic packet scheduling algorithm for load balancing in a multi-hop relay-enhanced cellular ofdma-tdd system. In *14th Asia-Pacific Conference on Communications, 2008. APCC 2008.*, pages 1 –5, October. 2008.

[103] Tariq M. King, Djuradj Babich, Jonatan Alava, Peter J. Clarke, and Ronald Stevens. Towards self-testing in autonomic computing systems. In *Eighth International Symposium on Autonomous Decentralized Systems, 2007. ISADS '07.*, pages 51 –58, March 2007.

[104] Heribert Kirschfink. Collective traffic control on motorways, August 1999.

[105] Jana Koehler, Chris Giblin, Dieter Gantenbein, and Rainer Hauser. On autonomic computing architectures. In *IBM Research*, 2003.

[106] Bastian Koller and Lutz Schubert. Towards autonomous sla management using a proxy-like approach. *Multiagent Grid Syst.*, 3(3):313–325, August 2007.

[107] Derrick Kondo, Gilles Fedak, Franck Cappello, Andrew A. Chien, and Henri Casanova. Characterizing resource availability in enterprise desktop grids. *Future Generation Computer Systems*, 23(7):888 – 903, 2007.

[108] Klaus Krauter, Rajkumar Buyya, and Muthucumaru Maheswaran. A taxonomy and survey of grid resource management systems for distributed computing. *Software: Practice and Experience*, 32(2):135–164, 2002.

[109] David P. Kreil. From general scientific workflows to specific sequence analysis applications: The study of compositionally biased proteins. *PhD thesis*, 2001.

[110] Hannes Kulovits, Christoph Stoegerer, and Wolfgang Kastner. System Architecture for Variable Message Signs. In *Proceedings 10th IEEE International Conference on Emerging Technologies and Factory Automation*, pages 903 – 909, 2005.

[111] D. Davide Lamanna, James Skene, and Wolfgang Emmerich. Slang: a language for defining service level agreements. In *Proceedings of The Ninth IEEE Workshop on Future Trends of Distributed Computing Systems, 2003. FTDCS 2003.*, pages 100 – 106, May 2003.

[112] Ben Langmead, Cole Trapnell, Mihai Pop, and Steven Salzberg. Ultrafast and memory-efficient alignment of short DNA sequences to the human genome. *Genome Biology*, 10(3):R25, 2009.

[113] Bu Sung Lee, Shixing Yan, Ding Ma, and Guopeng Zhao. Aggregating iaas service. In *2011 Annual SRII Global Conference (SRII)*, pages 335–338, April 2011.

[114] Cynthia Bailey Lee and Allan Snavely. On the user-scheduler dialogue: Studies of user-provided runtime estimates and utility functions. *International Journal of High Performance Computer Applications*, 20(4):495–506, 2006.

[115] Kevin Lee, Norman W. Paton, Rizos Sakellariou, and Alvaro A. A. Fernandes. Utility driven adaptive workflow execution. In *Proceedings of the 2009 9th IEEE/ACM International Symposium on Cluster Computing and the Grid*, CCGRID '09, pages 220–227, 2009.

[116] Young Choon Lee, Chen Wang, Albert Y. Zomaya, and Bing Bing Zhou. Profit-driven service request scheduling in clouds. In *10th IEEE/ACM International Conference on Cluster, Cloud and Grid Computing (CCGrid), 2010*, pages 15–24, may. 2010.

[117] Chunlin Li and Layuan Li. Competitive proportional resource allocation policy for computational grid. *Future Generation Computer Systems*, 20(6):1041–1054, 2004.

[118] Heng Li, Bob Handsaker, Alec Wysoker, Tim Fennell, Jue Ruan, Nils Homer, Gabor Marth, Goncalo Abecasis, Richard Durbin, and 1000 Genome Project Data Processing Subgroup. The sequence alignment/map format and samtools. *Bioinformatics*, 25(16):2078–9, 2009.

[119] Paul Lin, Alexander MacArthur, and John Leaney. Defining autonomic computing: a software engineering perspective. In *Proceedings of 2005 Australian Software Engineering Conference, 2005.*, pages 88–97, April 2005.

[120] Burkhard Linke, Robert Giegerich, and Alexander Goesmann. Conveyor: a workflow engine for bioinformatic analyses. *Bioinformatics*, 27(7):903–911, 2011.

[121] Antonios Litke, Kleopatra Konstanteli, Vassiliki Andronikou, Sotirios Chatzis, and Theodora Varvarigou. Managing service level agreement contracts in OGSA-based grids. *Future Generation Computer Systems*, 24(4):245–258, 2008.

[122] Wenjie Liu and Zhanhuai Li. Research and design of autonomic computing system model in cloud computing environment. In *2011 International Conference on Multimedia Technology (ICMT)*, pages 5025–5028, July 2011.

[123] Xin Lu and Zilong Gu. A load-adapative cloud resource scheduling model based on ant colony algorithm. In *2011 IEEE International Conference on Cloud Computing and Intelligence Systems (CCIS)*, pages 296–300, September 2011.

[124] Zaigham Mahmood. Cloud computing: Characteristics and deployment approaches. In *2011 IEEE 11th International Conference on Computer and Information Technology (CIT)*, pages 121–126, September 2011.

[125] Josef Makolm. A holistic reference framework for e-government: The practical proof of a scientific concept. In *Proceedings of the 39th Annual Hawaii International Conference on System Sciences, 2006. HICSS '06.*, volume 4, page 77, January 2006.

[126] Murugesan Malathi. Cloud computing concepts. In *2011 3rd International Conference on Electronics Computer Technology (ICECT)*, volume 6, pages 236–239, April 2011.

[127] Emmanuel Marilly, Oliver Martinot, Helene Papini, and Danny Goderis. Service level agreements: a main challenge for next generation networks. In *2nd European Conference on Universal Multiservice Networks, 2002. ECUMN 2002.*, pages 297–304, 2002.

[128] Majed Al Mashari, Z. Irani, and Mohamed Zairi. Holistic business process reengineering: an international empirical survey. In *Proceedings of the 34th Annual Hawaii International Conference on System Sciences, 2001.*, page 10 pp., January 2001.

[129] Mathew L. Massie, Brent N. Chun, and David E. Culler. The Ganglia distributed monitoring system: Design, implementation and experience. *Parallel Computing*, 30(7):817–840, 2004.

[130] Toni Mastelic, Vincent C. Emeakaroha, Michael Maurer, and Ivona Brandic. M4cloud - generic application level monitoring for resource-shared cloud environments. In *2nd International Conference on Cloud Computing and Services Science (CLOSER 2012)*, April 2012.

[131] Michael Maurer, Ivona Brandic, Vincent C. Emeakaroha, and Schahram Dustdar. Towards knowledge management in self-adaptable clouds. In *Proceedings of the 2010 6th World Congress on Services*, SERVICES '10, pages 527–534, 2010.

[132] Michael Maurer, Ivona Brandic, and Rizos Sakellariou. Simulating autonomic sla enactment in clouds using case based reasoning. In *ServiceWave 2010: Proceedings of the 2010 ServiceWave Conference*, Ghent, Belgium, 2010.

[133] Michael Maurer, Ivona Brandic, and Rizos Sakellariou. Enacting slas in clouds using rules. In *Proceedings of the 17th international conference on Parallel processing - Volume Part I*, Euro-Par'11, pages 455–466, 2011.

[134] Michael Maurer, Ivan Breskovic, Vincent C. Emeakaroha, and Ivona Brandic. Revealing the mape loop for the autonomic management of cloud infrastructures. In *International Workshop on Management of Cloud Systems (MoCS 2011), in association with the IEEE Symposium on Computers and Communications (ISCC 2011)*, pages 147–152, June 2011.

[135] Rajat Mehrotra, Abhishek Dubey, Sherif Abdelwahed, and Weston Monceaux. Large scale monitoring and online analysis in a distributed virtualized environment. In *2011*

8th IEEE International Conference and Workshops on Engineering of Autonomic and Autonomous Systems (EASe), pages 1 –9, april 2011.

[136] Peter Mell and Tim Grance. The nist definition of cloud computing. *National Institute of Standards and Technology*, 53(6):50, 2009.

[137] Daniel A. Menascé. TPC-W: A benchmark for e-commerce. *IEEE Internet Computing*, 6(3):83–87, 2002.

[138] Shicong Meng, Srinivas R. Kashyap, Chitra Venkatramani, and Ling Liu. Remo: Resource-aware application state monitoring for large-scale distributed systems. In *Proceedings of the 2009 29th IEEE International Conference on Distributed Computing Systems*, ICDCS '09, pages 248–255, 2009.

[139] Nirav Merchant, John Hartman, Sonya Lowry, Andrew Lenards, David Lowenthal, and Edwin Skidmore. Leveraging cloud infrastructure for life science research laboratories: A generalized view. In *International Workshop on Cloud Computing at OOPSLA09*, Orlando, USA, 2009.

[140] Joseph Cosmas Mushi, Guan zheng Tan, Felix Musau, and Cheruiyot Wilson. Modeling m-saas delivery model for threshold-based credit recharging using m-banking. In *2011 3rd International Conference on Computer Research and Development (ICCRD)*, volume 2, pages 307 –311, march 2011.

[141] Daniel Nurmi, Rich Wolski, Chris Grzegorczyk, Graziano Obertelli, Sunil Soman, Lamia Youseff, and Dmitrii Zagorodnov. The eucalyptus open-source cloud-computing system. In *Proceedings of the 2009 9th IEEE/ACM International Symposium on Cluster Computing and the Grid*, CCGRID 2009, pages 124–131, 2009.

[142] Oracle. Oracle virtualization. http://www.oracle.com/us/technologies/virtualization/index.html (Last Access: April 3, 2012).

[143] Suraj Pandey, Linlin Wu, Siddeswara Mayura Guru, and Rajkumar Buyya. A particle swarm optimization-based heuristic for scheduling workflow applications in cloud computing environments. In *AINA '10: Proceedings of the 2010 24th IEEE International Conference on Advanced Information Networking and Applications*, pages 400–407, Washington, DC, USA, 2010. IEEE Computer Society.

[144] Long-Tae Park, Jong-Wook Baek, and J. Woon-Ki Hong. Management of service level agreements for multimedia internet service using a utility model. *IEEE Communications Magazine*, 39(5):100 –106, May 2001.

[145] Elizabeth Pennisi. Will computers crash genomics? *Science*, 331(6018):666–668, 2011.

[146] Mark Perry and Halina Kaminski. Sla negotiation system design based on business rules. In *IEEE International Conference on Services Computing, 2008. SCC '08.*, volume 2, pages 609 –612, july 2008.

[147] Radu Prodan and Simon Ostermann. A survey and taxonomy of infrastructure as a service and web hosting cloud providers. In *10th IEEE/ACM International Conference on Grid Computing, 2009*, pages 17 –25, October 2009.

[148] Jian Pu, Kin F. Li, Mostofa Akbar, Gholamali C. Shoja, and Eric Manning. A reliable sla-based admission controller for mpls networks. In *IFIP International Conference on Network and Parallel Computing Workshops, 2007*, pages 57 –64, September 2007.

[149] Massimiliano Rak, Salvatore Venticinque, Tam´s M´hr, Gorka Echevarria, and Gorka Esnal. Cloud application monitoring: The mosaic approach. In *2011 IEEE Third International Conference on Cloud Computing Technology and Science (CloudCom)*, pages 758 –763, 29 2011-dec. 1 2011.

[150] Jan S. Rellermeyer, Gustavo Alonso, and Timothy Roscoe. Building, deploying, and monitoring distributed applications with eclipse and r-osgi. In *Proceedings of the 2007 OOPSLA workshop on eclipse technology eXchange*, eclipse '07, pages 50–54, 2007.

[151] S. Reyes, C. Muoz-Caro, A. Nio, R. Sirvent, and R.M. Badia. Monitoring and steering grid applications with grid superscalar. *Future Generation Computer Systems*, 26(4):645 – 653, 2010.

[152] Gene E. Robinson, Jody A. Banks, Dianna K. Padilla, Warren W. Burggren, C. Sarah Cohen, Charles F. Delwiche, Vicki Funk, Hopi E. Hoekstra, Erich D. Jarvis, Loretta Johnson, Mark Q. Martindale, Carlos Martinez Del Rio, Monica Medina, David E. Salt, Saurabh Sinha, Chelsea Specht, Kevin Strange, Joan E. Strassmann, Billie J. Swalla, and Lars Tomanek. Empowering 21st century biology. *BioScience*, 60(11):923–930, 2010.

[153] B. Rochwerger, D. Breitgand, E. Levy, A. Galis, K. Nagin, I. M. Llorente, R. Montero, Y. Wolfsthal, E. Elmroth, J. Cáceres, M. Ben-Yehuda, W. Emmerich, and F. Galán. The reservoir model and architecture for open federated cloud computing. *IBM J. Res. Dev.*, 53(4):535–545, July 2009.

[154] Paolo Romano. Automation of in-silico data analysis processes through workflow management systems. *Briefings in Bioinformatics*, 9(1):57–68, October 2007.

[155] Florian Rosenberg, Christian Platzer, and Schahram Dustdar. Bootstrapping performance and dependability attributes ofweb services. In *Proceedings of the IEEE International Conference on Web Services*, ICWS '06, pages 205–212, 2006.

[156] Mohsen Salehi and Rajkumar Buyya. Adapting market-oriented scheduling policies for cloud computing. In *Algorithms and Architectures for Parallel Processing*, volume 6081 of *Lecture Notes in Computer Science*, pages 351–362. Springer Berlin / Heidelberg, 2010.

[157] SalesForce. Service cloud. http://www.salesforce.com/ (Last Access: April 3, 2012).

[158] Laura Savu. Cloud computing: Deployment models, delivery models, risks and research challenges. In *2011 International Conference on Computer and Management (CAMAN)*, pages 1 –4, May 2011.

[159] SAX. Simple API for XML. http://sax.sourceforge.net/ (Last Access: April 3, 2012).

[160] Sena Seneviratne and David C. Levy. Task profiling model for load profile prediction. *Future Generation Computer Systems*, 27(3):245 – 255, 2011.

[161] Jin Shao and Qianxiang Wang. A performance guarantee approach for cloud applications based on monitoring. In *2011 IEEE 35th Annual Computer Software and Applications Conference Workshops (COMPSACW)*, pages 25 –30, july 2011.

[162] Jin Shao and Qianxiang Wang. A performance guarantee approach for cloud applications based on monitoring. In *2011 IEEE 35th Annual Computer Software and Applications Conference Workshops (COMPSACW)*, pages 25 –30, July 2011.

[163] Zhang Shu and Song Meina. An architecture design of life cycle based sla management. In *The 12th International Conference on Advanced Communication Technology (ICACT), 2010*, volume 2, pages 1351 –1355, February 2010.

[164] Kornel Skalkowski, Jakub Sendor, Renata Slota, and Jacek Kitowski. Application of the esb architecture for distributed monitoring of the sla requirements. In *Proceedings of the 2010 Ninth International Symposium on Parallel and Distributed Computing*, pages 203–210, 2010.

[165] Damian Smedley, Morris A. Swertz, Katy Wolstencroft, Glenn Proctor, Michael Zouberakis, Jonathan Bard, John M. Hancock, and Paul Schofield. Solutions for data integration in functional genomics: a critical assessment and case study. *Briefings in Bioinformatics*, 9(6):532–544, September 2008.

[166] Borja Sotomayor, Rubén S. Montero, Ignacio M. Llorente, and Ian Foster. Virtual infrastructure management in private and hybrid clouds. *IEEE Internet Computing*, 13(5):14–22, 2009.

[167] Vijayaraghavan Soundararajan and Kinshuk Govil. Challenges in building scalable virtualized datacenter management. *SIGOPS Operating System Review*, 44:95–102, December 2010.

[168] Brikena Statovci-Halimi, Artan Halimi, K. Hendling, and Harmen R. van As. A framework for dynamic sla management under heterogeneous traffic conditions in mpls networks. In *Proceedings of the 2003 IEEE International Performance, Computing, and Communications Conference*, pages 217 – 224, April 2003.

[169] Lincoln D. Stein. Towards a cyberinfrastructure for the biological sciences: progress, visions and challenges. *Nature Reviews Genetics*, 9(9):678–688, 2008.

[170] Christoph Stoegerer and Wolfgang Kastner. System management standards for traffic management systems. In *Proceedings of the 14th IEEE Conference on Emerging Technologies and Factory Automation (EFTA 09)*, pages 1–8, 2009.

[171] Christoph Stoegerer and Wolfgang Kastner. Approaches for increasing availability of component-based traffic management software. In *Proceedings of the 13th IEEE Conference on Intelligent Transportation Systems (ITSC 10)*, pages 1608 – 1613, 2010.

[172] Christoph Stogerer, Ivona Brandic, Vincent C. Emeakaroha, Wolfgang Kastner, and Thomas Novak. Applying availability slas to traffic management systems. In *14th International IEEE Conference on Intelligent Transportation Systems (ITSC), 2011*, pages 1501 –1506, October 2011.

[173] Ali Tehraninasr and Edris Heidari Darani. Business process reengineering: A holistic approach. In *International Conference on Information and Financial Engineering, 2009. ICIFE 2009.*, pages 79 –82, April 2009.

[174] Abhishek Tiwari and Arvind K.T. Sekhar. Workflow based framework for life science informatics. *Computational Biology and Chemistry*, 31(5-6):305 – 319, 2007.

[175] Cole Trapnell, Lior Pachter, and Steven L. Salzberg. Tophat: discovering splice junctions with RNA-Seq. *Bioinformatics*, 25(9):1105–1111, 2009.

[176] Luis M. Vaquero, Luis Rodero-Merino, Juan Caceres, and Maik Lindner. A break in the clouds: towards a cloud definition. *SIGCOMM Computer Communication Review*, 39:50–55, December 2008.

[177] Srikumar Venugopal, James Broberg, and Rajkumar Buyya. OpenPEX: An open provisioning and execution system for virtual machines. In *Proceedings of the 17th International Conference on Advanced Computing and Communications (ADCOM'09)*, 2009.

[178] Arnupharp Viratanapanu, Ahmad Kamil Abdul Hamid, Yoshihiro Kawahara, and Tohru Asami. On demand fine grain resource monitoring system for server consolidation. In *Kaleidoscope: Beyond the Internet? - Innovations for Future Networks and Services, 2010 ITU-T*, pages 1 –8, December 2010.

[179] Thomas Voith, Karsten Oberle, Manuel Stein, Eduardo Oliveros, Georgina Gallizo, and Roland Kubert. A path supervision framework a key for service monitoring in infrastructure as a service (iaas) platforms. In *Proceedings of the 2010 36th EUROMICRO Conference on Software Engineering and Advanced Applications*, SEAA '10, pages 127–130, 2010.

[180] Chien-Min Wang, Hsi-Min Chen, Chun-Chen Hsu, and Jonathan Lee. Dynamic resource selection heuristics for a non-reserved bidding-based grid environment. *Future Generation Computer Systems*, 26(2):183 – 197, 2010.

[181] Miao Wang, Viliam Holub, Trevor Parsons andJohn Murphy, and Patrick O'Sullivan. Scalable run-time correlation engine for monitoring in a cloud computing environment. In *2010 17th IEEE International Conference and Workshops on Engineering of Computer Based Systems (ECBS)*, pages 29 –38, March 2010.

[182] John M. Wilson. An algorithm for the generalized assignment problem with special ordered sets. *Journal of Heuristics*, 11(4):337–350, 2005.

[183] Maria Wimmer and Bianca von Bredow. E-government: aspects of security on different layers. In *Proceedings. 12th International Workshop on Database and Expert Systems Applications, 2001.*, pages 350 –355, 2001.

[184] Maria Wimmer and Bianca von Bredow. A holistic approach for providing security solutions in e-government. In *Proceedings of the 35th Annual Hawaii International Conference on System Sciences, 2002. HICSS.*, pages 1715 – 1724, January 2002.

[185] Matthias Winkler, Thomas Springer, and Alexander Schill. Automating composite sla management tasks by exploiting service dependency information. In *IEEE 8th European Conference on Web Services (ECOWS), 2010*, pages 59 –66, December 2010.

[186] Timothy Wood, Prashant Shenoy, Arun Venkataramani, and Mazin Yousif. Sandpiper: Black-box and gray-box resource management for virtual machines. *Comput. Netw.*, 53(17):2923–2938, December 2009.

[187] Min-You Wu, Wei Shu, and H. Zhang. Segmented min-min: a static mapping algorithm for meta-tasks on heterogeneous computing systems. In *Proceedings of 9th Heterogeneous Computing Workshop, 2000. (HCW 2000)*, pages 375 –385, 2000.

[188] Ming Xia, M. Batayneh, Lei Song, C.U. Martel, and B. Mukherjee. Sla-aware provisioning for revenue maximization in telecom mesh networks. In *IEEE Global Telecommunications Conference, 2008. IEEE GLOBECOM 2008.*, pages 1 –5, December 2008.

[189] Guofu Xiang, Hai Jin, Deqing Zou, Xinwen Zhang, Sha Wen, and Feng Zhao. Vmdriver: A driver-based monitoring mechanism for virtualization. In *2010 29th IEEE Symposium on Reliable Distributed Systems*, pages 72 –81, November 2010.

[190] Zan Xiao and Donggang Cao. A policy-based framework for automated sla negotiation for internet-based virtual computing environment. In *2010 IEEE 16th International Conference on Parallel and Distributed Systems (ICPADS)*, pages 694 –699, December 2010.

[191] Shixing Yan, Bu Sung Lee, Guopeng Zhao, Ding Ma, and Mohamed P. Infrastructure management of hybrid cloud for enterprise users. In *2011 5th International DMTF Academic Alliance Workshop on Systems and Virtualization Management (SVM)*, pages 1 –6, October 2011.

[192] Bo Yang, Xiaofei Xu, Feng Tan, and Dong Ho Park. An utility-based job scheduling algorithm for cloud computing considering reliability factor. In *2011 International Conference on Cloud and Service Computing (CSC)*, pages 95 –102, December 2011.

[193] Zhi Yang, Changqin Yin, and Yan Liu. A cost-based resource scheduling paradigm in cloud computing. In *2011 12th International Conference on Parallel and Distributed Computing, Applications and Technologies (PDCAT)*, pages 417 – 422, October 2011.

[194] Chee Shin Yeo and Rajkumar Buyya. Pricing for utility-driven resource management and allocation in clusters. *International Journal of High Performance Computer Applications*, 21(4):405–418, 2007.

[195] Cao Yuanming, Wang Wendong, Gong Xiangyang, and Que Xirong. Initiator-domain-based sla negotiation for inter-domain qos-service provisioning. In *Fourth International Conference on Networking and Services, 2008. ICNS 2008.*, pages 165 –169, March 2008.

[196] Hongjiang Zhang and Wei-Ying Ma. Adaptive content delivery on mobile internet across multiple form factors. In *Proceedings of 10th International Multimedia Modelling Conference, 2004.*, page 8, January 2004.

[197] Shuai Zhang, Shufen Zhang, Xuebin Chen, and Xiuzhen Huo. Cloud computing research and development trend. In *Second International Conference on Future Networks, 2010. ICFN '10.*, pages 93 –97, January 2010.

[198] Gansen Zhao, Chunming Rong, Martin Gilje Jaatun, and Frode Eika Sandnes. Deployment models: Towards eliminating security concerns from cloud computing. In *2010 International Conference on High Performance Computing and Simulation (HPCS)*, pages 189 –195, July 2010.

[199] Zhenxing Zhao, Congying Gao, and Fu Duan. A survey on autonomic computing research. In *2009. PACIIA 2009. Asia-Pacific Conference on Computational Intelligence and Industrial Applications*, volume 2, pages 288 –291, November 2009.

[200] Hai Zhong, Kun Tao, and Xuejie Zhang. An approach to optimized resource scheduling algorithm for open-source cloud systems. In *2010 Fifth Annual ChinaGrid Conference (ChinaGrid)*, pages 124 –129, July 2010.

[201] Jiantao Zhou, Shang Zheng, Delin Jing, and Hongji Yang. An approach of creative application evolution on cloud computing platform. In *Proceedings of the 2011 ACM Symposium on Applied Computing*, SAC '11, pages 54–58, New York, NY, USA, 2011. ACM.

[202] Farhana Zulkernine, Patrick Martin, Chris Craddock, and Kirk Wilson. A policy-based middleware for web services sla negotiation. In *IEEE International Conference on Web Services, 2009. ICWS 2009.*, pages 1043 –1050, July 2009.

Glossary

ActiveMQ *Apache ActiveMQ* - A powerful open source message broker, which fully implements the java message service. 21

AEF *Automated Emulation Framework* - A tool originally designed for automated configuration and execution of emulated experiments. However, it works also as a virtualized infrastructure manager to set up virtual machines in virtualized environments. 28

CASViD *Cloud Application SLA Violation Detection* - An architecture capable of monitoring single customer applications to determine their performance status and thereby check for SLA violation situations in an environment, where multiple customer applications are deployed on the same host. 44

CEP *Complex Event Processing* - is a technology to process events and discover complex patterns among multiple streams of event data. 22

Cloud *Cloud Computing* - facilitates the implementation of scalable on-demand computing infrastructures combining concepts from virtualization, Grid, and distributed system. It provisions resources and applications in a pay-as-you-go manner, where the customer pays only what it consumed. 1

CloudSim *Cloud Simulation tool* - is a scalable simulation engine that supports the modeling and simulation of large scale Cloud computing environments including data centers on single computing machine. It also supports the modeling of service brokers, resource provisioning, and application allocation policies. 40

CPU *Central Processing Unit* - The brain of a computer, which contains the circuitry necessary to interpret and execute program instructions. 18

DeSVi *Detecting SLA Violation infrastructure* - An architecture for monitoring Cloud resources and detecting SLA violations of applications executing alone on virtual machines. It is also capable of determining optimal measurement interval for carrying out the monitoring operations. 26

DSL *Domain Specific Language* - is a small language used to define specific domain problems. 17

ESP *Event Stream Processing* - deals with the task of processing multiple streams of event data with the goal of identifying the meaningful events within those streams and deriving meaning information from them. 22

FoSII *Foundations of Self-governing ICT Infrastructures* - A research project funded by the Vienna Science and Technology Fund known in german as Wiener Wissenschafts-, Forschungs und Technologiefonds (WWTF). It proposes models and concepts for autonomic SLA management and enforcement in Clouds. 9

Grid *Grid Computing* - combines computers from multiple administrative domains to reach a common goal, such as to solve a single task, and may then disappear just as quickly. 1

HPC *High Performance Computing* - is the use of parallel processing for running advanced computation intensive application programs efficiently, reliably, and quickly. 78

IaaS *Infrastructure as a Service* - is a Cloud delivery model where the customer has full access and uses fundamental computing resources such as CPU and storage. The customer can fully control the operating system and hardware devices. 2

JMS *Java Message Service* - A Java message oriented middleware API for distributed communication of messages between clients. 21

KM *Knowledge Management* - In our context, it means intelligent usage of measured data obtained by monitoring for the decision making process to guarantee application performance goals defined in SLA agreement while optimizing computational resource usages. 52

LoM2HiS *Low-level Metric to High-level SLA* - A novel framework for monitoring Cloud infrastructure resources and mapping the low-level resource metrics to the equivalence of the high-level SLA parameters. 15

MAPE *Monitoring, Analysis, Planning, Execution* - An intelligent closed loop of control used by autonomic managers to manage devics' states and behaviours in autonomic environment. 13

MIB *Management Information Base* - a text file in the standard SNMP format that defines the individual objects one can manage with common SNMP tools. 46

MIPS *Millions Instruction Per Second* - is a unit used to simulate the utilization of CPU. Its conversion is based on the assumption that an Intel Xeon(R) 3 GHz processor delivers 10000 MIPS for 100% resource utilization of one core. 94

MTBF *Mean Time Between Failure* - It denotes the time the system was operational between the last system failure and the next. 19

MTTR *Mean Time To Repair* - It denotes a time it takes to bring a system back online after a failure situation. 19

MySQL A relational database management system that can run as a standalone server providing access to multi-users and multiple databases. 22

NGS *Next Generation Sequencing* - A recently introduced high-throughput technology for the identification of nucleotides molecules like RNA in biomedical samples. 54

PaaS *Platform as a Service* - A Cloud delivery model that provides a hosting environment for the customer application. The customer has the ability to fully control its applications. However, it has limited control of the operating system, hardware, and network devices of the hosting environment. 2

POV-Ray *Persistence of Vision Raytracer* - A ray tracing program available for a variety of computer platforms. It can be used to create high-quality three-dimension graphics. 67

QoS *Quality of Service* - A collection of metrics to specify the performance requirements of a service. 12

RNA *Ribonucleic Acid* - It is a nucleic acid molecule similar to DNA but containing ribose rather than deoxyribose. 51

SaaS *Software as a Service* - is a Cloud delivery model where customers use a Cloud application but cannot control the operating system, hardware, and network devices in the environment. 1

SAM *Sequence Alignment/Map* - A tool used to provide various utilities for manipulating RNA sequence alignment including sorting, merging, indexing, and generating alignments in a per-position format. 92

SAX *Simple API for XML* - A simple parser that provides mechanism for reading out data from an XML document. 21

SCP *Secure Copy Protocol* - It is a protocol based on secure shell that uses a simple Public Key infrastructure and Encryption to allow users to exchange files securely between unix host. 31

SLA *Service Level Agreement* - can be defined as a contract between a Cloud provider and a customer describing functional and non-functional characteristics of a service including QoS requirements, penalties in case of violations, and a set of metrics, which are used to measure the provisioning of the requirements. 12

SLO *Service Level Objective* - specifies the objectives of the service level agreement parameters. 13

SNMP *Simple Network Management Protocol* - It is a standard TCP/IP network protocol used to monitor and control data traffics. It uses agents to collect data, which are then passed to the manager. 45

SQL *Structured Query Language* - is a programming language designed for managing data in relational database management systems. It was initially developed at IBM in the early 1970s 22

SSH *Secure Shell* - It is a unix-based commandline interface protocol that allow data to be transferred using a secure channel between two networked devices. 31

TMS *Traffic Management Systems* - are tools used to retrieve information from traffic fields as well as propagate information to traffic participants. They consist of many subsystems built up in a hierarchical structure of components. 22

TopHat is a fast splice junction mapper for RNA-Seq reads. It aligns RNA-Seq reads to mammalian-sized genomes using the ultra high-throughput short read aligner Bowtie, and then analyzes the mapping results to identify splice junctions between exons. 53

TPC-W is a transactional web performance benchmark. Its workload is performed in a controlled internet commerce environment that simulates the activities of a business oriented transactional web server. 67

TT *Threat Threshold* - is a value that is more stricter than the service level objective value. Exceeding this value indicates a threat of violating the real SLA objective values. 58

VM *Virtual Machine* - is a software implementation of a computer that executes programs like a physical machine. It does not physically exist but it provides the same resource interfaces as physical machines however, they vary in performance. 28

Xen is a virtualization technology for creating virtual machines on physical machine and managing their deployments. 68

XML *eXtensible Markup Language* - is a metalanguage that allows users to describe structured data. 21

i want morebooks!

Buy your books fast and straightforward online - at one of world's fastest growing online book stores! Environmentally sound due to Print-on-Demand technologies.

Buy your books online at

www.get-morebooks.com

Kaufen Sie Ihre Bücher schnell und unkompliziert online – auf einer der am schnellsten wachsenden Buchhandelsplattformen weltweit! Dank Print-On-Demand umwelt- und ressourcenschonend produziert.

Bücher schneller online kaufen

www.morebooks.de

VDM Verlagsservicegesellschaft mbH
Heinrich-Böcking-Str. 6-8　　Telefon: +49 681 3720 174　　info@vdm-vsg.de
D - 66121 Saarbrücken　　　Telefax: +49 681 3720 1749　　www.vdm-vsg.de

Printed by Books on Demand GmbH, Norderstedt / Germany